BCPL – the language and its compiler

To Pat and Pat

BCPL – the language and its compiler

Martin Richards
Computer Laboratory, University of Cambridge

Colin Whitby-Strevens
Inmos Ltd, Bristol

The right of the
University of Cambridge
to print and sell
all manner of books
was granted by
Henry VIII in 1534.
The University has printed
and published continuously
since 1584.

Cambridge University Press

Cambridge
London   New York   New Rochelle
Melbourne   Sydney

Published by the Press Syndicate of the University of Cambridge,
The Pitt Building, Trumpington Street, Cambridge CB2 1RP
32 East 57th Street, New York, NY 10022, USA
10 Stamford Road, Oakleigh, Melbourne 3166, Australia

First published 1980
First paperback edition 1982
Reprinted 1982, 1984, 1985

Printed in Great Britain by J. W. Arrowsmith Ltd, Bristol

Library of Congress catalogue card number: 77–91098

British Library Cataloguing in Publication Data

Richards, Martin
BCPL, the language and its compiler.
1. *BCPL (Computer program language)*
I. Title   II. Whitby-Strevens, Colin
001.64′24   *QA*76.73.*B*17
ISBN 0 521 21965 5 *hard covers*
ISBN 0 521 28681 6 *paperback*

Contents

Foreword   ix

1   The BCPL philosophy   1
1.1   Introduction   1
1.2   The object machine   1
1.3   Variables and manifest constants   2
1.4   Data types   2
1.5   Syntax of BCPL   3
1.6   Modularity   4
1.7   Portability   5
1.8   Summary   5

2   The main features of BCPL   7
2.1   Introduction   7
2.2   A simple BCPL program   7
2.3   Variables and variable declarations   8
2.4   Constants   9
2.5   More input and output   11
2.6   The if-command, relational operators, compound commands   13
2.7   Repetitive commands   14
2.8   The for-command   16
2.9   Arithmetic   17
2.10   TEST and UNLESS; conditional expressions   17
2.11   Vectors   20
2.12   Procedures   21
2.13   Strings, and vectors of characters   23
2.14   Local and global variables   25
2.15   The switchon-command   27
2.16   Conclusions   29

3   Advanced facilities   30
3.1   Pointers   30
3.2   The use of pointers   31
3.3   Handling conceptual data types   34
3.4   Procedure parameters   35
3.5   Recursion   36
3.6   Scope rules: who knows about what   38
3.7   Other controls   38

3.8   Bit-operations 39
3.9   Goto-commands and labels 41
3.10   Typeless names – or context type determination 42
3.11   Procedures as values 42
3.12   Static variables 44
3.13   Separate compilation facilities 45

4   The library, language extensions, and machine independence 47
4.1   Basic input and output procedures 47
4.2   Input and output library facilities 48
4.3   Miscellaneous 52
4.4   LEVEL and LONGJUMP 52
4.5   APTOVEC 54
4.6   Freestore management 55
4.7   The floating-point extension 57
4.8   The field-selector extension 57
4.9   The infixed byte operator 58
4.10   Techniques for machine independence and portability 58

5   Debugging and error handling 60
5.1   Syntax errors 60
5.2   Semantic errors 62
5.3   Runtime error handling 62
5.4   BACKTRACE, MAPSTORE, and ABORT 63
5.5   TRACE and the profile option 67
5.6   DEBUG: an interactive debugging system 67
5.7   Runtime potholes and traps 74

6   The BCPL lexical and syntax analyser 79
6.1   The lexical analyser 80
6.2   The function LOOKUPWORD 90
6.3   Miscellaneous lexical analysis procedures 94
6.4   The applicative expression tree 98
6.5   RDBLOCKBODY, RDSEQ, RDCDEFS, and RDSECT 106
6.6   The analysis of expressions 110
6.7   The analysis of definitions 116
6.8   The analysis of commands 118

7   Compiler portability 124
7.1   Introduction 124
7.2   OCODE 125
7.3   The code generator 130
7.4   The bootstrapping process and INTCODE 133

8   Language definition   145
8.1   Program   145
8.2   Elements   145
8.3   Expressions   146
8.4   Section brackets   150
8.5   Commands   150
8.6   Declarations   155
8.7   Miscellaneous features   160
8.8   The formal syntax of BCPL   161

        References   167
        Index   169

Foreword

BCPL was designed by one of the authors in 1967 (Richards [10]). It underwent substantial development over the next five years, but since then has remained relatively stable. It is a small language aimed primarily at systems-programming applications. Its compiler is portable, and, as a result, it has over the years been implemented on a large number of machines worldwide. We admit to not knowing exactly how many different implementations currently exist, but we know of ones for at least twenty-five different machines.

BCPL is used for a wide variety of systems-programming applications, ranging over operating systems, compilers and interpreters, data-base packages, simulators, text processors and editors, algebra systems, and many others. It is used in undergraduate courses as a vehicle for teaching systems programming.

This book has been written with several distinct purposes in mind. Firstly, it aims to provide an introduction to the language for people who are experienced programmers but have not met it before; secondly, it is designed as a handbook for established BCPL users; thirdly, it will be valuable for those planning to transfer BCPL to a new machine; and last, but by no means least, it contains much supporting material for courses concerned with compiler writing.

In serving these diverse needs, the book includes for the newcomer an informal introduction to the language (chapter two) and a chapter on debugging and error handling (chapter five). As the user gains experience, the language is discussed in greater depth in chapters three and four, and chapter eight forms the reference manual.

We feel that it is necessary to study substantial programs written in a language in order to learn how to use the language effectively and to develop a good programming style. For this reason a number of extended examples have been included in the book. In particular, the whole of chapter six is devoted to a description of the BCPL syntax analyser, which is a carefully written program that well exhibits the power of the language.

Finally, chapter seven addresses portability issues, outlining the mechanism used for transferring the BCPL compiler to a new machine.

Acknowledgements

This book reflects the work of many people besides the authors. In particular, chapter two is strongly influenced by Brian Kernighan's C-tutorial [6] and chapter eight is based on a manual written by J. H. Morris [8], itself based on a well-written memorandum by R. H. Canaday and D. M. Richie [5]. Chapter seven contains some material that was previously published in *Software portability* [4]. Many BCPL users, too numerous to acknowledge individually, have contributed much by means of suggestion, advice and comment (particularly in the section on potholes and traps in chapter five!). However, we are especially grateful to Ken Moody and David May who have made countless useful comments on the early drafts of the book. Finally, we are indebted to Charles Lang for his interest, encouragement and support.

August 1979
Cambridge and Leamington Spa

1

The BCPL philosophy

1.1 Introduction

The language BCPL (Basic CPL) was originally developed as a compiler-writing tool and, as its name suggests, is closely related to CPL (Combined Programming Language) which was jointly developed at Cambridge and London Universities. CPL is described in Barron *et al.* [1]. BCPL adopted much of the syntactic richness of CPL, and strives for the same high standard of linguistic elegance; however, in order to achieve the efficiency necessary for systems-programming, its scale and complexity is far less than that of CPL. The most significant simplification is that BCPL has only one data type – the bit-pattern – and this feature alone gives it a characteristic flavour which is quite different from that of CPL and most other current programming languages.

BCPL has proved itself to be useful as a compiler-writing and systems-programming tool. It has been implemented on a wide range of computers, both large and small, and has been used for research and teaching computer science as well as systems programming.

1.2 The object machine

BCPL has a simple semantic structure which is based on an idealised machine. This design was chosen to make BCPL both portable and easy to define accurately.

The most important feature of the idealised object machine is its *store*, which consists of a set of numbered storage cells arranged so that the numbers labelling adjacent cells differ by one. Each storage cell holds a bit-pattern, called simply a *value*. All storage cells are of the same size (a constant of the implementation, which is usually between 16 and 36 bits). A value that can be stored in a cell is the only kind of object that can be manipulated directly in BCPL, and every variable and expression in the language will always evaluate to one of these values.

Values are used by the programmer to model abstract objects of many different kinds, such as numbers, truth values, strings and functions. Many basic operations on values are provided. One of these, of fundamental importance in the object machine, is *indirection*. This operation takes one operand which is interpreted as

1

an integer and it yields the contents of the storage cell labelled by that integer. This operation is assumed to be efficient and, as will be seen later, the programmer may use it freely in his BCPL program.

1.3 Variables and manifest constants

A *variable* in BCPL is defined to be a name which has been associated with a storage cell. It has a value, the contents of the cell, which can be changed by an assignment command during execution. Almost all forms of definition in BCPL introduce variables, the only exception being the manifest constant declaration.

A *manifest constant* is the direct association of a name with a value. This association takes place at compile time and remains constant throughout execution. There are many situations where manifest constants can be used to improve readability with no loss of runtime efficiency.

1.4 Data types

The unusual way in which BCPL treats data types is fundamental to its design. It is convenient to distinguish between two classes of data types, namely, conceptual types and internal types. The *conceptual type* of an expression is the kind of abstract object the programmer had in mind when he wrote the expression. It might be, for instance, a time in milliseconds, a weight in grams, a function to transform feet per second to miles per hour, or it might be a data structure representing an employee record. It is, of course, impossible to enumerate all the conceptual types that could exist and it is equally impossible to provide for all of them within a programming language. The usual practice when designing a language is to select from the conceptual types a few basic ones and provide a suitable internal representation together with enough basic operations. The term *internal type* refers to any one of these basic types, and the intention is that all the conceptual types can be modelled effectively using the internal types. A few of the internal types provided in a typical language are real, integer, Boolean, character, label, function, etc.

Much of the flavour of BCPL is the result of the conscious design decision to provide only one internal type, namely the bit-pattern, which we simply refer to as a value. In order to allow the programmer to model any conceptual type, many useful primitive operations have been provided. For instance, the ordinary arithmetic operators $+$, $-$, $*$, and $/$ have been defined in such a way as to model the integer operations directly. One may think of these operations as ones which interpret their operands as integers, performing integer arithmetic; alternatively one may think of them as operations which work directly on bit-patterns and just happen to be useful for working with integers. This latter approach is closer to the BCPL philosophy. Although the BCPL programmer has direct access to the bits comprising a value, the details of the binary representation used to represent integers are not defined and he would lose machine independence if he performed non-numerical operations on values he knows to represent integers. Standard relational operators have been defined and a complete set of bit-manipulation operations provided. In addition, there are some stranger bit-pattern operations which provide ways of representing functions, labels, vectors and structures. All these operations are efficient and each can be translated into just a few instructions for most machines.

The most important effects of designing the language in this way can be summarised as follows:

1. There is no need for type declarations in the language, since the internal type of every variable is already known. This helps to make programs concise and also simplifies problems such as the handling of actual/formal parameter correspondence and separate compilation.

2. It gives the language nearly the same power as one with dynamically varying types, and yet retains the efficiency of a language (like Fortran) with manifest types. Although the internal type of an expression is always known by the compiler, its conceptual type can never be. It may, for instance, depend on the values of variables within the expression, such as the value of an index to an element of a vector, since such elements are not necessarily all of the same conceptual type. It should be noted that in languages (such as Algol) where the elements of arrays must all have the same type, one needs some other linguistic device in order to handle dynamically varying data structures.

3. Since there is only one internal type in the language there can be no automatic type checking, and it is possible to write nonsensical programs which the compiler will translate without complaint. This disadvantage has to be weighed against the simplicity, power and efficiency that this treatment of types makes possible.

1.5 Syntax of BCPL

One of the design criteria of BCPL was that it should be a useful systems-programming tool and it was felt that high readability was of extreme importance. The readability of a program largely depends on the skill and style of the programmer; however his task is simplified if he is using a language with a rich set of expressive but concise constructions and if all the syntactic details of the language have been carefully thought out.

Readability is aided by using a character set which contains both capital and small letters. Many implementations expect capital letters to be used in reserved words, but allow lower-case letters to be used in user-introduced names for contrast. Any number of characters can be used in an identifier and all are significant.

The structure of a BCPL program can be simple and direct. The programmer is able to retain explicit control at all times. The compiler treats the program simply (and often naively), and the object code produced is always a direct result of what the programmer writes, without the introduction of hidden overheads.

In BCPL there are three basic commands: assignments, routine commands and jumps. However, there are a large number of syntactic constructions to control the flow of control in an algorithm, considerably reducing (to zero in many cases) the need for labels and goto-commands, and consequently improving readability.

The purpose of a *declaration* in BCPL is threefold: (*a*) to introduce a name and specify its scope; (*b*) to specify its extent; (*c*) to specify its initial value. The *scope* of a name is the textual region of program in which it may be used to reference the same data item; this region is usually a block or the body of a routine. The *extent* of a variable is the time through which it exists and is associated with a storage cell.

In BCPL, variables may be divided into two classes:

1. *Static variables*. The extent of a static variable is the entire execution time of the program. The storage cell is allocated prior to execution and continues to exist until execution is complete.

2. *Dynamic variables*. A dynamic variable is one whose extent starts when its declaration is executed and continues until execution leaves the scope of the variable. Dynamic variables are usually necessary when using routines recursively.

The class of variable depends on the form of declaration used. There are six ways of declaring static variables and four ways of declaring dynamic variables.

An *expression* is used primarily for the computation of the value that it yields and is syntactically distinct from a *command* whose purpose is the effect that it has, such as the updating of a variable by assignment, when it is executed. There is a corresponding distinction between *functions* and *routines*, namely that a function application is an expression and yields a value, whereas a routine call is a command and does not. Since a function is so similar to a routine in most other respects, the word *procedure* is used to mean either in contexts where the distinction is unimportant. All procedures may be used recursively, and in order to allow for this and yet maintain very high execution efficiency, there is the restriction that the free variables of a procedure (i.e. variables declared outside it) must be static.

1.6   Modularity

With efficient procedure calls, it is good practice to design programs in a modular fashion. For example, each module could contain the procedures operating on a conceptual data type, through which all manipulations would be performed, without fear of the inefficiencies this approach often brings with it. BCPL uses a form of static storage, called the *global vector*, which allows separately compiled modules to reference and call each other and to share data. This facility is not unlike the Fortran Common storage area. In general, the combination of these features leads to a better programming style and eases the programming management problems.

Separate compilation also provides the basis for library facilities. Most implementations provide a set of precompiled procedures, each associated with a separate location in the global vector. The compiler itself knows nothing of the procedures contained in the runtime system, yet all the user has to do is to ask the compiler to scan a standard file of global declarations.

1.7   Portability

The compiler itself is written in BCPL and has been transported from machine to machine many times. It is easy to write portable BCPL programs, if a few simple guidelines are followed (see chapter four). The compiler is written to operate in three phases; the end product of the first two is a machine-level program which operates on the idealised BCPL machine. The third phase has to be rewritten for each implementation and translates the program for the idealised machine into one for the available hardware. In addition a small runtime system (possibly as small as 100 machine instructions) has to be written.

The specially written third phase of the compiler can be compiled and run on an existing BCPL implementation and, when preceded by the first two phases on that machine, results in a *cross-compiler*. The full compiler can now be recompiled, resulting in a proper compiler for the new machine. Implementing BCPL on a new machine takes, typically, about two or three man-months.

Most of the standard BCPL library is also written in BCPL, so this too can be used as a basis for compatibility between machines, and for the inevitable installation-dependent extensions.

1.8   Summary

The way in which BCPL treats data types allows the programmer great freedom to organise his symbol tables, property lists, tree structures and stacks in the most suitable fashion for his own application. Admittedly BCPL only provides the basic operations and the programmer has to write his own manipulative routines, but this is easy to do and he does not have the disadvantage of having to use a system in which inappropriate design decisions have already been made. The philosophy of BCPL is not one of the tyrant who thinks he knows best and lays down the law on what is and what is not allowed; rather, BCPL acts more as a servant offering his services to the best of his ability without complaint, even when confronted with apparent nonsense. The programmer is always assumed to know what he is doing and is not hemmed in by petty restrictions. Machine-code programmers tend to like the way in which BCPL combines the advantages of a high-level language with the ability to use addresses and bit-patterns without invoking a great weight of expensive machinery.

When planning and writing software in a commercial environment, it is necessary to compromise between the quality of a product and its cost. The quality is affected by many factors such as its size, its speed and efficiency, the usefulness of its error diagnostics, its robustness and reliability, the accuracy and quality of its documentation, its maintainability, and in some cases its flexibility and mobility. Only the first two of these are directly improved by writing in a more efficient language, while the others tend to suffer from this because the software is more difficult to write. Although efficiency is important in a systems-programming language, this consideration should not wholly dominate its design. The compromise in the design of BCPL between efficiency and linguistic effectiveness is near optimal for a wide range of software applications, especially those in which flexibility is required.

2

The main features of BCPL

2.1 Introduction

This chapter is a self-contained introduction for the newcomer to the language. Not all the features are covered, and many fine details are skipped. The aim is to present the major constructs and to communicate the flavour of programming in BCPL. Chapter eight provides a precise and complete, though necessarily terse, specification of the language. You will also need the local implementation notes giving details of dialect representations and how to compile and run BCPL programs.

This chapter assumes that you are familiar with job control, file creation and editing, etc. in your local operating system and that you have programmed in some language before.

2.2 A simple BCPL program

A BCPL program consists of one or more procedure declarations (which are similar to the functions and subroutines of Fortran or the procedures of Algol or PL/I), perhaps preceded by some global-variable declarations. One of the procedures must be called START, and program execution commences by calling it. In turn it will usually call on other procedures to perform its job, some in the same program, others included from libraries. A very simple declaration of START might be as follows:

```
LET START() BE WRITES("Hello, World")
```

The straightforward way of communicating data between procedures is by using parameters. The parameter list is placed in parentheses following the procedure's name in the declaration. Here START is a procedure with no parameters, indicated by ( ).

A procedure is invoked by writing its name, followed by the list of arguments in brackets. There is no call-statement as in Fortran or PL/I. WRITES is a library procedure which will print a string on the terminal (or some other output device,

e. g. a printer for offline jobs etc., depending upon the implementation environment). In this case it prints

```
Hello, World
```

To make it into a complete program, it is necessary to declare the library
procedures at its head. These declarations are usually stored for your convenience
on a system library file, which you incorporate into your program using a
get-directive. So the complete program would be as follows:

```
GET "LIBHDR"
LET START( ) BE WRITES("Hello, World")
```

The actual name of the file will, of course, depend on your
installation.

2.3   Variables and variable declarations

This program adds three integers and prints their sum:

```
GET "LIBHDR"
LET START( ) BE
        $( LET A, B, C, SUM =  1, 2, 3, Ø
           SUM := A + B + C
           WRITES("Sum is ")
           WRITEN(SUM)
        $)
```

*[handwritten: ? needs WRITES (" *N") to make ST execute WRITEN N ?]*

The *section brackets* $(and $) enclose the statements of a procedure, and are, in
many respects, like **begin** and **end** in Algol. Statements are usually separated
either by a semicolon or by the end of the line.

The let-declaration is used to introduce program variables as well as procedures. All variables must be declared before they are used (i.e. their names
written in commands etc.). The declaration

```
LET A, B, C, SUM = 1, 2, 3, 0
```

introduces four new *local variables* A, B, C and SUM and initialises them to contain 1,
2, 3 and zero respectively.

Variable names may have any number of characters, chosen from A–Z, Ø–9 and
. (full stop), but must start with a letter. The basic words of the language (e.g. LET)
cannot be used as variable names. Various implementations allow lower-case
letters and/or use an underline character instead of a full stop.

BCPL does not have the type-association conventions for variables that are found in many languages (e.g. integer, real, character, Boolean). It is up to you what 'type' of information you store in the variables of your program. However, many of the various operations that you can perform will make assumptions about the contents of your variables. For example, the +, as in A+B, adds together the contents of the variables A and B, making the assumption that they contain integers and that an integer result is required.

Assignment commands are much the same as in Algol, Fortran or PL/I. Note the use of : =. For simple arithmetic expressions, the usual operators (+, – etc.) are used. A longer treatment of expressions is given later; meanwhile be guided by your experience with other programming languages.

The library procedure WRITEN outputs its parameter as an integer.

BCPL programs are written in free format. You can put several statements on a single line, or use several lines for a single statement. Semicolons must be used to separate statements on a single line to resolve ambiguity and can also be included for greater clarity. 'end of line' has the effect of terminating a statement if syntactically this is possible. So if you want to split a statement over two lines, then the split may be at any point where the statement could not be terminated, for example after a + or –. Spaces and newlines may not be inserted in the middle of names or operators. However, as a matter of style, they should be used frequently to enhance readability.

Comments are introduced by the character pair //. All characters from (and including) // up to the end of the line are ignored by the compiler.

2.4 Constants

We have already seen *decimal integer constants* in the previous example. Constants may also be expressed in octal, introduced by the character #. Thus #777 is an *octal constant*, with decimal value 511.

A *character constant* is enclosed in single quotes and denotes the implementation-dependent small-integer value that represents that character. For example, 'A' = 65 on an ASCII implementation, and 'A' = 193 on an EBCDIC implementation. Ordinary variables may be used to store character constants, for example

```
LET CHAR =  'A'
```

A special mechanism is used to represent hard-to-get-at or invisible characters. This uses an asterisk followed by a printable character. The most common use of this mechanism is *N to represent the 'end of line' character. This is a special character which is produced at the end of each line of input and, when printed, moves the printing unit to the start of the next line. Other uses of the asterisk notation are *P for 'end of page', *S for space, *T for tab, *B for backspace, * ' for single quote mark and ** for * itself. Your implementation may have even more (depending on the character set used).

A valuable feature of BCPL to help you write in a clear programming style is the ability to use names to represent constants. These are called *manifest constants*. The value associated with a manifest constant stays fixed, so you cannot assign to it. The compiler knows the value, so it can generate efficient code. No extra store is wasted. Above all, it is much clearer to see what a program is doing if you use a well-chosen name instead of an an arbitrary number. Here is a skeleton of a program, not using manifest constants:

```
LET DAY = Ø
  .   .   .
DAY := 1
  .   .   .
DAY := 5
  .   .   .
```

We are obviously considering different days, but are they days of the week, or days since some specific date? All becomes clear when we rewrite the program using manifest constants:

```
MANIFEST $( SUNDAY = Ø; MONDAY = 1; TUESDAY = 2
            WEDNESDAY = 3; THURSDAY = 4; FRIDAY = 5
            SATURDAY = 6
         $)
LET DAY = SUNDAY
  .   .   .
DAY := MONDAY
  .   .   .
DAY := FRIDAY
  .   .   .
```

You should also make less mistakes when using manifest constants. In many of the program extracts used as examples throughout this book we will use manifest constants, assuming that appropriate declarations have been made earlier in the program.

Exercises I

1. Which of the following are legal BCPL variable names?

```
DAY    LET    2ND    TAX.RATE    TAX-RATE    .END
```

2. Which of the following are legal BCPL constants?

178 '*T' 'TT' '*' 26 #178 #Ø 'A' ' ' ' ' ' ' ' ' '

3. Correct the syntax errors in the following program:

```
LET START( BE
$(  LET A  B  C  := 1, 'A', 'B', #37
    MANIFEST  $(  SUM = A  $)
    SUM := SUM + A + B - C
    LET RESULT = 2 * SUM
    WRCH RESULT       $)
$)
```

4. Write a program to print your name, and run it on your local BCPL system.

2.5   More input and output

The BCPL input/output (I/O) system is based on the idea of streams. A BCPL *stream* should be regarded simply as a sequence of characters. There is no record structure superimposed by BCPL. Normally one input stream and one output stream are selected at any moment. All I/O operations take place on the currently selected input or output stream. However, the mechanism for specifying the original source and final destination is very much dependent on the operating environment. Usually a suitable set of defaults is provided so that simple use of BCPL has expected results.

To override these defaults, the SELECTINPUT library routine is used to select the stream from which subsequent input is to be taken. Similarly, SELECTOUTPUT selects the stream to which subsequent output is to be sent.

RDCH and WRCH form the basis of the BCPL I/O library. RDCH fetches one character from the currently selected input each time it is called, and returns that character as its value. RDCH yields the character '*N' at the end of each input line. When it reaches the end of the selected input, it returns a special value represented by the manifest constant ENDSTREAMCH (which will be defined in LIBHDR).

WRCH outputs one character to the currently selected output each time it is called. Successive calls on the output library procedures will place more characters onto the current line until the character '*N' is transferred. Thus

```
WRITES("This is")
WRITES(" line one*N")
```

will produce

```
This is line one
```

whereas the procedure call

```
WRITES("Each*Nword*Non*Na*Nline*N")
```

will produce

```
Each
word
on
a
line
```

Similarly, on input, characters are read one at a time as you ask for them. In illustrating this we introduce the input library function **READN**, which ignores all layout characters on the input stream up to the first digit. It then reads a number (terminated by a non-digit). The sequence

```
A := READN()
B := READN()
C := READN()
```

has the same effect if the input takes the form

```
1 2 3
```

or

```
1
2
3
```

When designing an interactive program, you should check whether your local BCPL system (and/or operating system) will permit character-by-character inter-action. On many systems, a complete line has to be typed before your BCPL program is allowed to read any characters. Equally, on output, you may find that each line is buffered by the system and will only appear on the terminal after your program has output a newline character.

2.6   The if-command, relational operators, compound commands

The main condition-testing statement in BCPL is the if-command:

```
C := RDCH()
IF C='?' THEN WRITES("Why did you type a questionmark?*N")
```

The condition to be tested is any expression. The word THEN is followed by a command. The expression is evaluated, and, if its value is true the command is executed. The representation of 'true' and 'false' is implementation dependent. If your expression does not evaluate to either true or false, then it is implementation sensitive whether the command is executed or not.

The character = is one of the relational operators in BCPL. Here is the complete set:

=	equal to (.EQ. to Fortraners)
¬=	not equal to
>=	greater than or equal to
<=	less than or equal to
>	greater than
<	less than

The *relational operator* performs an arithmetic comparison of the two expressions either side, and yields a Boolean result (true or false). You can write extended tests in BCPL, e.g.

```
C := RDCH()
IF '∅'<=C<='9' THEN PROCESS.DIGIT()
```

Here the procedure PROCESS.DIGIT is called if the character read was a digit. (N.B. this assumes that the digits have numerically consecutive representations in the character set).

Tests can be combined with the operators & (and), | (or) and ¬ (not). For example we can test whether a character is a space, tab or newline with

```
IF C='*S' | C='*T' | C='*N'  THEN . . .
```

BCPL provides a complementary command to IF, called UNLESS. This has the same format, but the command following is executed if the expression evaluates to false.

You can store truth values in any BCPL variable, so the following construct is both valid and meaningful:

```
T := A > B
  .   .   .
IF T THEN WRITES("A was greater than B when T was set")
```

One of the most useful features of BCPL is that one form of command is a set of statements enclosed in a $($) pair. As a simple example, suppose that we wish to ensure that A is bigger than B, as part of a sort procedure. The interchange of A and B takes three statements in BCPL, which can be grouped together as a unit by $(and $):

```
IF A < B  THEN
    $(   LET T = A
         A := B;   B := T
    $)
```

As a general rule in BCPL, anywhere that you can write a simple command, you can use a compound command or a block. The set of statements enclosed in $($) is called a *compound command* unless the statements start with some declarations, in which case the whole thing is called a *block*.

$(and $) are called *section brackets*. BCPL has a feature which allows section brackets to be tagged with identifiers. The compiler attempts to match the tags on corresponding pairs of opening and closing section brackets. If necessary, a tagged closing section bracket will automatically cause extra section brackets to be inserted immediately preceding it, closing off inner sections.

The ability to replace single statements by complex ones at will is one feature that makes BCPL much more pleasant to use than, say, Fortran. Logic (like the exchange in the previous example) which would require GOTOs and labels in Fortran can, and should, be written in BCPL without any, using compound commands and blocks.

Compound commands should not be allowed to grow too large. Your program's comprehensibility can often be increased by using more procedures and fewer blocks provided that the names of the procedures are chosen carefully. Every few lines of a properly constructed program will have a name which states its purpose. If your program seems to take the form of just a large number of blocks, then look at it carefully to see if parts of it can be logically separated.

2.7   Repetitive commands

BCPL has a range of repetitive commands. First we introduce **WHILE** and **REPEATWHILE**. The following is an extract from the **READN** library routine (described in detail in chapter four):

```
WHILE 'Ø'<=CH<='9' DO
          $( SUM := 1Ø * SUM + CH - 'Ø'
             CH := RDCH()  $)
```

The while-command is a loop whose general form is

WHILE expression DO command

Its meaning is

(a) evaluate the expression
(b) if its value is true, execute the command and go back to (a)

Because the expression is tested before the command is executed, the command can be executed zero times. This feature is often desirable. As in the if-statement, the expression and the command can both be arbitrarily complicated. In the example, CH is tested for a character value representing a digit. If so, the accumulated number value is multiplied by 10 and the numerical value of the digit added in. The next character is read, and the process repeated for as long as the 'next' character satisfies the test for a digit.

Sometimes it is desirable to perform the testing after the execution of the command, not before, ensuring that the command is obeyed at least once. For this we can use REPEATWHILE, as in this extract, also from READN:

```
CH := RDCH() REPEATWHILE CH='*S' |
                         CH='*T' |
                         CH='*N'
```

The general form of the repeatwhile-command is

command REPEATWHILE expression

Its meaning is

(a) execute the command
(b) evaluate the expression, if it is true then go back to (a)

In this extract, each character is tested for *S, *T or *N after it has been read from the input. If the test succeeds then another character is read. This is used in READN to ignore leading layout characters.

There are three other looping commands with similar formats:

```
UNTIL expression DO command
command REPEATUNTIL expression
command REPEAT
```

The until- and repeatuntil-commands act similarly to while- and repeatwhile-commands, except that they loop if the expression is false. The statement

```
command REPEAT
```

is equivalent to

```
command REPEATWHILE TRUE
```

This construction is in practice very useful when used in conjunction with various loop-exiting facilities (described later). An example of this is given in section 2.12.

2.8   The for-command

The for-command includes the initialisation and increment parts of the loop together at the start of the loop. The two alternative forms are

```
FOR N = expression1 TO expression2 BY constant-expression
                    DO command
```

and

```
FOR N = expression1 TO expression2 DO command
```

A new variable N is declared and initialised to expression1. It is then tested against expression2 to see if the for-command should be terminated. If not, the command is executed and N is incremented by constant-expression (assumed equal to 1 if not present). The test is then performed again, and so on.

Several properties of FOR should be noted. Firstly, the step-length must be a constant (or constant-expression). Secondly, N can be used within the controlled command (you can assign to it if you really want to – this will interfere with the number of times the loop is executed) but it cannot be accessed outside the whole construction. It is a new variable (different from any other variable N in the program) and it exists only for the duration of the for-command. It is referred to as the *controlled variable*. Thirdly, expression1 and expression2 are evaluated only at the beginning of the command, not each time round the loop. Fourthly, if constant-expression is positive, then the test is made to see if N is greater than expression2, but if constant-expression is negative, the test is made to see if N is less than expression2.

2.9 Arithmetic

The arithmetic operators are +,−,* (multiplication), / (truncating integer division), and the remainder (or modulo) operator REM.

```
FOR I = Ø TO COUNT DO
        $( IF I REM 8 = Ø THEN WRCH('*N')
           WRITEN(I)
                      .   .   .
        $)
```

In this example a newline is output every eight times round the loop for layout purposes. Integer representation is implementation dependent, and overflow in arithmetic operations is ignored in BCPL. All the arithmetic operators work on integers and the results of / and REM are implementation dependent unless both operands are positive.

2.10 TEST and UNLESS; conditional expressions

The test-command is a variation of the if-command, allowing you to specify one of two alternative commands to be obeyed. Here are the two commands for comparison:

```
IF    expression THEN command1
TEST expression THEN command1 ELSE command2
```

There is also a third from:

```
UNLESS expression DO command2
```

The effect of these is as follows: The expression is evaluated. A true evaluation results in command1 being executed (for IF and TEST), whereas a false evaluation results in command2 being executed (for TEST and UNLESS). Thus to set X to the minimum of A and B we may write

```
TEST A < B THEN X := A ELSE X := B
```

The words THEN and DO are synonyms, and usually may be omitted.

BCPL provides an alternative form of conditional which is often more concise. It is called the *conditional expression* as it is a conditional which produces a value, and it can be used anywhere an expression is allowed. The value of

```
A<B  -> C, D
```

is C if A is less than B, otherwise it is D. The general form is

```
expression1 -> expression2, expression3
```

This means
  (*a*) evaluate expression1
  (*b*) if expression1 is true, then the value of the whole conditional expression is
        expression2, otherwise it is expression 3.
  To set X to the minimum of A and B we can now write

```
X := A<B -> A, B
```

This can be extended in an obvious manner to find the minimum of A, B and C, i.e.

```
X := A<B -> A<C -> A, C,
          B<C -> B, C
```

In the following example, which is an extract from the **WRITEF** library routine, it is desired to set N to the integer value represented by the hexadecimal character in CH:

```
N := 'Ø'<=CH<='9' -> CH - 'Ø',
                 1Ø + CH - 'A'
```

If N contains a digit, then the required value is obtained by subtracting the value of the character 'Ø', otherwise it is obtained by adding 10 and subtracting the value of the character 'A'.
  Test-commands can be used for constructions that branch in one of several ways and then rejoin (a common programming structure) as follows:

```
TEST    . . .
   THEN    . . .
   ELSE  TEST   . . .
            THEN    . . .
            ELSE  TEST   . . .
                     THEN   . . .
                     ELSE   . . .
```

The conditions are tested in order and exactly one alternative is executed. This will be the first one whose `TEST . . . THEN` is satisfied. When this alternative has finished, the next statement to be executed is the one after the one following the final `ELSE`. If no action is to be taken should none of the tests be satisfied, then the final `TEST . . . THEN . . . ELSE` should be changed to `IF . . . THEN . . .`

As a final example of the use of `TEST` and `IF`, the following extract from the BCPL syntax analyser (described in full in chapter six) checks that tagged section brackets are correctly matched:

```
TEST TAG = WORDNODE
    THEN NEXTSYMB( )
    ELSE IF WORDNODE=NULLTAG THEN
            $( SYMB := Ø
               SYNREPORT(9)    $)
```

Exercise II

1. (*a*) Write a BCPL program that will copy input to output on a character-by-character basis.

(*b*) Modify your program to condense multiple spaces into a single space and multiple newlines into a single newline.

(*c*) Modify your program so that trailing spaces are removed and blank lines omitted.

2. Write a program to merge two input streams of sorted numbers.

3. Write a program fragment that has the same effect as the for-command, but using `LET` and `UNTIL`. Check your answer with chapter eight, page 152.

4. What is the effect of each of the following for-commands?
   (*a*) `FOR I = J TO J+2 DO J := J + 1`
   (*b*) `FOR I = 5 TO Ø DO . . .`
   (*c*) `FOR I = -5 TO -3 DO . . .`
   (*d*) `FOR I = 1 TO 5 DO I := I + 1`

5. Is the following BCPL program ambiguous?

```
IF A THEN TEST B THEN IF C THEN P( ) ELSE Q( )
```

Under what conditions is the call on: (*a*) P executed; (*b*) Q executed; (*c*) both P and Q executed; (*d*) neither P nor Q executed? Write these conditions as BCPL expressions.

2.11   Vectors

In BCPL, as in many other programming languages, it is possible to set up an array of elements accessed using only one variable name. Only one-dimensional arrays are provided in BCPL, and they are called *vectors*. You can make a vector of four elements with the declaration

```
LET V = VEC 3
```

Many programming languages use parentheses or [ ] to enclose subscripts, but in BCPL the operator ! is used to provide a compact notation which distinguishes subscription from procedure calls. Subscripts begin at zero, and the elements of V are

V!Ø, V!1, V!2 and V!3

The character ! is usually pronounced by BCPL users as 'pling' in this context. ! takes a precedence over other operators, so parentheses are required if the subscript is a compound expression. For example

V!I+J does not mean V!(I+J)
but (V!I)+J

   As an example, the following routine outputs a positive number, storing the individual digits in a vector:

```
LET WRITEPN(N) BE
$(   LET T = VEC 2Ø
     LET I = Ø
     T!I, N, I := N REM 1Ø, N/1Ø, I+1 REPEATUNTIL N=Ø
     FOR J = I - 1 TO Ø BY -1 DO WRCH(T!J + 'Ø')
$)
```

   Note that in the LET V = VEC . . . declaration you write the maximum subscript. This must be a constant, so you can't let your program choose the size of the vector. You can, however, write a constant-expression, involving constants and some operators. For example, if ROWS and COLUMNS are manifest constants you can write

```
LET V = VEC ROWS*COLUMNS
```

   As with ordinary variables, you can imagine that the contents of the vector's elements are of any type you choose. However, note that, unlike ordinary variables, there is no way of initialising the contents of a vector when it is declared. In general each element of a vector will contain non-zero rubbish until you assign a value to it.

Another warning about vectors: you should not try to use the same name for a vector and an ordinary variable, and should only use the vector's name without a subscript with the greatest of care (e.g. passing the vector as a parameter as in Algol) until you understand the section on pointers in chapter three. It is both legal and full of pitfalls for the unwary.

2.12   Procedures

Suppose we wish, as part of a large program, to form a histogram of the integers less than 100 (terminated by a negative integer) on some input stream. Let us also count all larger integers. Since this is an isolated part of the program, good practice dictates making it a separate procedure. Here is one way:

```
GET "LIBHDR"
MANIFEST $( NUM = 1ØØ $)
LET START() BE
  $( LET HISTOGRAM = VEC NUM
     .   .   .
     COUNT(HISTOGRAM, NUM)  //  form histogram
     WRITES(  .  .  .  )
     .   .   .
  $)

AND COUNT(ARRAY, SIZE) BE
$( FOR I = Ø TO SIZE DO
            ARRAY!I := Ø    //  all counts set to zero
   $( LET C = READN()       //  read next number
      IF C < Ø RETURN       //  input terminated by neg number
      IF C>SIZE THEN C := SIZE // deal with large numbers
      ARRAY!C := ARRAY!C + 1
   $) REPEAT
$)
```

We have seen many examples of calling procedures, so let us concentrate on how to define one. COUNT has two parameters, ARRAY and SIZE. These are called the *formal parameters* of the procedure. When COUNT is called, they will be passed the values of the corresponding *actual parameters* used in the call. Note that we do not have to mention that ARRAY is a vector. The fact that we use it as such within the procedure is good enough for BCPL. However, it is the programmer's responsibility to make sure that if a parameter is treated as a vector inside a procedure, then a vector is provided in the procedure call.

The effect of the parameter-passing mechanism in BCPL is that simple variables are passed by value, and vectors by reference. Thus the routine COUNT can access the elements of the vector HISTOGRAM by using the ! operator on the parameter ARRAY. However, SIZE can be regarded as a local variable, initialised to the value of the corresponding actual parameter (in this case 100, the value of NUM). The actual parameters can, in general, be expressions.

The return-command simply says 'go back to the calling procedure'. If RETURN is the last command of the procedure, then it can be omitted.

The LET procedure-definition
        AND procedure-definition

construction is simply a method of defining two procedures simultaneously. Usually you can access only those procedures declared either simultaneously with or prior to the calling procedure. In this case we used AND and so were able to call COUNT from within START, although the procedure was defined textually later in the program.

If we wish to return a value at the end of forming the histogram, then COUNT has to become a function, and is defined as a value-returning object producing a result:

```
LET COUNT(ARRAY, SIZE) = VALOF
   $( LET NUMBER = Ø
      FOR I = Ø   TO SIZE DO ARRAY!I := Ø
      $(  LET C = READN()
          IF C<Ø RESULTIS NUMBER
          IF C>SIZE THEN C := SIZE
          ARRAY!C := ARRAY!C + 1
          NUMBER := NUMBER + 1   //  count the numbers
      $)  REPEAT
   $)
```

The block following VALOF is executed in the normal way until a command of the form

```
RESULTIS expression
```

is met. This expression then produces the value for the whole function. In fact the construction

```
VALOF  $(  . . .
              RESULTIS expression
          $)
```

can be used to produce a value anywhere a value is needed (e.g. on the right-hand side of an assignment command). An expression can be used as the body of a function definition; for example, to define the function which yields the minimum of three values we can write

```
LET MIN(A, B, C) = A<B -> A<C -> A, C,
                    B<C -> B, C
```

The parameter-passing mechanism in BCPL contains a subtlety which can trap unsuspecting programmers used to other programming languages. As simple variables are passed by value, a copy is made of the actual parameters for the called procedure to use. Assigning to the formal parameters will not change the values of the original variables specified as actual parameters. This is similar to the Algol call-by-value mechanism, and in contrast to the Fortran parameter-passing mechanism.

BCPL has been carefully designed so that function and routine calls bring little overhead. This is a by-product of the lack of parameter checking and the fact that all parameters are passed by value. By using routines properly, you will increase readability, save space taken up by compiled code, produce better modularity, all at little cost in terms of runtime overhead.

2.13   Strings, and vectors of characters

Text may be stored in a vector using one element for each character. However, we usually need only between 6 and 9 bits for each character while a store location may be anything from 16 to 64 bits wide (both character size and word size depend on implementation). Plainly it is far more economical to store text by placing several characters in each word. BCPL strings are stored in this way.

In BCPL, we use double quotes around a character string. The compiler permanently allocates a vector of store into which it packs the string. The BCPL value of the string is, in fact, the address of the first word of the vector. This value can be assigned like any other. Thus

```
S   :=   "My string"
WRITES(S)
```

has the same output effect as

```
WRITES("My string")
```

Sometimes it is necessary to access the individual characters of a string, and you will find a pair of library procedures called GETBYTE and PUTBYTE are provided to help you. Alternatively you can use UNPACKSTRING to lay a string out in a vector one character to a word, and PACKSTRING to pack it up again. After unpacking your string, you will discover that the first word contains a count of the number of characters in the string proper, which starts at the second word.

As an example, we give the library routines WRITES, UNPACKSTRING and PACKSTRING:

```
LET WRITES(S) BE
    FOR I = 1 TO GETBYTE(S,Ø) DO WRCH(GETBYTE(S,I))
LET UNPACKSTRING(S,V)  BE
    FOR I = Ø TO GETBYTE(S,Ø) DO V!I := GETBYTE(S,I)
LET PACKSTRING(V, S) = VALOF
$(  LET N = V!Ø & #XFF // extract least significant 8 bits
    LET SIZE = N / BYTESPERWORD
    S!SIZE := Ø          // pack out last word with zeroes
    FOR I = Ø TO N DO PUTBYTE(S, I, V!I)
    RESULTIS SIZE
$)
```

For both PACKSTRING and UNPACKSTRING two parameters are needed, one giving the string to be operated upon, the other a vector for the result. From this example you will have noticed that packed strings are stored in perfectly ordinary vectors. If you quote a string in your program, then the compiler automatically allocates a vector for it. However, you have to supply your own vectors for the PACKSTRING and UNPACKSTRING procedures.

The following extract from the BCPL lexical analyser is used as part of the table initialisation program (for full details see chapter six). It takes a string of the form "WORD1/WORD2/WORD3/.../WORDn//", and, for each word in turn, forms a string and calls the lookup procedure LOOKUPWORD. The vectors CHARV and WORDV are assumed declared, and the original string is identified by WORDS.

```
LET I, LENGTH = 1, Ø
$(  LET CH = GETBYTE(WORDS, I)
    TEST CH='/' THEN $( IF LENGTH = Ø THEN RETURN
                        CHARV!Ø := LENGTH
                        WORDSIZE := PACKSTRING(CHARV, WORDV)
                        LOOKUPWORD()
                          .   .   .
                        LENGTH := Ø      $)
                   ELSE $( LENGTH := LENGTH + 1
                           CHARV!LENGTH := CH      $)
    I := I + 1
$) REPEAT
```

Exercises III

1. Complete the histogram program outlined in section 2.12, and run it on some suitable data.

2. Explain what happens on the call of PACKSTRING from within the following program fragment:

```
LET V = VEC 3
V!Ø, V!1, V!2, V!3 := 3, 'A', 'B', 'C'
PACKSTRING(V, V)
```

The final word containing the string is padded out with zeroes. This allows strings to be compared for equality on a word-by-word basis. (For an example of this, see LOOKUPWORD in the BCPL lexical analyser, described in chapter six.) Discuss whether it is worth modifying the definition of PACKSTRING so that it acts sensibly for the above program.

3. Write a program to read some suitable piece of text and count the occurrences of A, AN, AND, ANDY, THAN, HAND and HANDY, treating each as (*a*) distinct words; (*b*) character strings (i.e. so that HAND increments the counts for A, AN, AND and HAND).

2.14 Local and global variables

Consider the following pair of procedures:

```
LET F() BE
  $( LET X, Y = Ø, Ø
     .  .  .
     G()
     .  .  .
  $)
AND G() BE
  $( LET X = Ø
     .  .  .
  $)
```

The three variables X and Y in F, and X in G are local to their own procedures. The X in F is unrelated to the X in G. Furthermore all three variables have no memory from one call to the next of the encapsulating procedures and are initialised to the stated value on each entry. They are often referred to as *dynamic variables*.

A further crucial point to note is that the dynamic variables of one procedure cannot be used in an embedded procedure:

```
LET  F() BE
  $(  LET X = Ø
      LET G() BE
          $(   .  .  .  //  X cannot be used in here
          $)
          .  .  .            //  but it can here
  $)
```

The technical way of expressing this rule is to say that BCPL does not support dynamic free variables; in other words, inner procedures are not permitted to use the dynamic variables of outer procedures. You should probably avoid using inner procedures in your initial attempts at using BCPL, and so avoid this problem altogether.

As opposed to local variables, *global variables* (*globals*) are potentially available to all procedures. The BCPL mechanism is to store all global variables in a special *global vector*, in a fixed place in store. The purpose of the global vector is to permit communication between separately compiled modules of a BCPL program (see chapter three). The program refers to the global variables by name in the usual way, but first there must be a declaration specifying which name goes with which location within the global vector. For this purpose, the locations in the global vector are numbered (usually from zero). In each installation some globals will be reserved for library procedures, so by convention you should avoid allocating these to your own global variables. Typically you can use locations from 100 upwards in the global vector.

To associate a name with a global-vector location (and hence create a global variable), a global-declaration is used. The declaration:

```
GLOBAL $( NUMBER:1ØØ; COUNTER:1Ø1    $)
```

associates NUMBER and COUNTER with locations 100 and 101 in the global vector. They may subsequently be used anywhere in the block containing the global-declaration, including embedded functions and procedures. The newcomer to BCPL is advised to declare all global variables together at the start of the program. Note that if you declare a variable called NUMBER as a local variable of some block then you introduce a new variable, rendering the global of that name temporarily inaccessible.

Much of the contents of the standard header file (here called LIBHDR) contains the global-declarations for the standard precompiled library files. The exact mechanism for combining program modules and the library procedures is obviously dependent on the operating environment.

In some implementations, extra directives are required to state which library procedures should be incorporated; e.g. a program might start

```
GET "LIBHDR"
NEEDS  RDCH, WRCH, WRITES
```

Without such a mechanism, the whole of a possibly substantial library would have to be incorporated into every program. Check with your installation notes for details.

2.15   The switchon-command

The switchon-command provides an elegant and efficient alternative to multiway testing using if- or test-commands. When tests are like this,

```
TEST C='a' THEN  . . .
ELSE TEST C='b' | C='c' THEN . . .
ELSE  .  .  .
```

where we are testing a computed value against a series of constants, then the switchon-command is often clearer and gives better compiled code. This example can be rewritten

```
SWITCHON C INTO
$(   //  the body of a SWITCHON is always a compound command
     //  you cannot put declarations here!!!
     CASE 'a':  . . .
               ENDCASE
     CASE 'b':
     CASE 'c':  . . .
               ENDCASE
     DEFAULT:   . . .     //  if none of the cases match
               ENDCASE
$)
//   ENDCASE  brings us here .
```

The case-labels are used to label the code defining the various actions we want. Readability is often enhanced by using manifest constants in case-labels. The label DEFAULT is used if none of the other cases contain the computed value of the expression following SWITCHON. DEFAULT is optional; if it is not there, and none of the cases match, then control passes directly to the next command after the switchon compound command.

The endcase-command says that the work of the switchon-command has been completed, and control is to be passed to the next command after the compound command. It is used because the case labels do not have the effect of terminating the previous case, i.e. after the statements at one label, control continues on to those textually following unless action is taken explicitly to escape. A further consequence of this simple approach is that it is possible to have multiple cases on a single statement, and it is possible to use other methods of transferring control other than ENDCASE.

The switchon-command is one of BCPL's aids to writing readable programs. However, it can be spoilt if each case label is attached to a large number of commands. Nine or ten lines of code should be the maximum. Where more are required, then they should be embedded in a routine which is called from the case-label (even if this is the only call to it in the whole program).

As an example, we give extracts from the compiler routine NEXTSYMB, which reads the next symbol from the input, setting the global SYMB to represent the symbol type. For the full text, see section 6.1.

```
LET NEXTSYMB() BE
$(1 NLPENDING := FALSE
$(2 . . .
    SWITCHON CH INTO
$(S CASE '*P':
    CASE '*N': LINECOUNT := LINECOUNT + 1
               NLPENDING := TRUE  //  ignorable characters
    CASE '*T':
    CASE '*S': RCH() REPEATWHILE CH='*S'
               LOOP
    CASE 'Ø':CASE '1':CASE '2':CASE '3':CASE '4':
    CASE '5':CASE '6':CASE '7':CASE '8':CASE '9':
               SYMB := S.NUMBER
               READNUMBER(1Ø)
               RETURN
                     .  .  .
    CASE '[':
    CASE '(': SYMB := S.LPAREN; BREAK
    CASE ']':
    CASE ')': SYMB := S.RPAREN; BREAK
                     .  .  .
$)S
$)2 REPEAT
    RCH()
$)1
```

2.16   Conclusion

This ends the discussion on the main features of BCPL. You now know enough to write quite substantial programs, and it would probably be a good idea if you paused long enough to do so. The next chapter will discuss some more constructions, useful but not essential.

Exercises IV

1. Write a program to show that the 13th day of the month falls more often on a Friday than any other day of the week. The 1st of January 1973 was a Monday. You should aim at producing the clearest possible program, not the fastest. (Hint: there are an exact number of weeks in four centuries.)

2. Write a program to generate primes in the range 1–1000 using the sieve of Eratosthenes. (Initialise a vector to contain the integers 1, 2, . . . , 1000. Consider each element in turn. If it is as initialised then it is prime, so print it and cancel all its multiples in the vector. If it is cancelled then it is not prime.)

3. Write a BCPL program to generate the first twenty terms in the Fibonacci series (1, 1, 2, 3, 5, 8, . . . , each term being the sum of the previous two terms), and to compute the ratio R of any two consecutive terms. 'Plot' the successive values of R on the output device.

3

Advanced facilities

In this chapter we will be discussing representations as well as facilities, and we shall be revisiting some of the features discussed in chapter two.

3.1 Pointers

A *pointer* in BCPL is the address of a word of store. It is rare indeed when we care what the specific address itself is, but pointers are commonly used to get at the contents of store. The unary operator ə is used to produce the address of a variable. Thus

```
LET A, B = Ø, Ø
B := əA
```

puts the address of A into the variable B. A has not changed in any way, and we can still access A by writing its name. However we can now also access A indirectly by applying the ! operator to B.

```
LET A, B, C = Ø, Ø, Ø
B := əA
C := !B
```

The construction !B means 'access the object pointed to by B'. The effect here is that we copy the contents of A into C. We could also change the contents of A by accessing it indirectly via B:

```
LET A, B = Ø, Ø
B   := əA
!B := 5
```

Here the effect is to put the value 5 into A, as it is the object pointed to by B.

In BCPL it is defined that consecutive words of store have numerically consecutive addresses. Thus if we know that B points to the first of several consecutive locations, then B+1 will point to the second location, B+2 to the third etc.

With this knowledge, we can explain BCPL vectors more fully. The declaration

```
LET V = VEC 5
```

establishes (i) a vector of six consecutive locations, and (ii) a separate variable V which is initialised to the address of the first location of the vector. Figure 3.1 shows a diagrammatic represention of this.

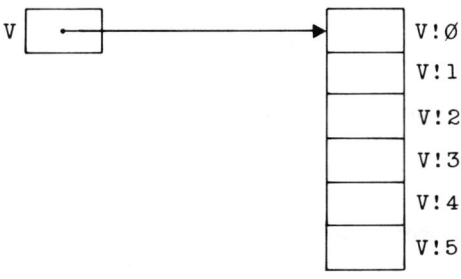

Fig. 3.1

V points to the first element of the vector. This means that the value given by V + 1 is the address of the second element of the vector. Hence to access this element we should write

```
!(V+1)
```

This would work, but, simply because this is rather cumbersome, the shorthand V!1 is used.

In this example, V behaves like any other local variable, the main difference being that it is initialised by the compiler as a pointer. Hence its value can be copied into another variable (which as a result will also point to the same vector), or passed as a parameter to a procedure.

3.2   The use of pointers

There are two other important uses of pointers to represent BCPL language constructs. The first is that the value of a string is a pointer to the vector in which the string is stored. Thus we could write the assignment command

```
VEGETABLE := "carrot"
```

and then

```
WRITES(VEGETABLE)
```

Note that in compiling a string the compiler does not allocate an extra variable to hold the address of the first word of store containing the string.

A *table* is an initialised, permanently allocated vector. The value of a *table* is a BCPL pointer to the first element of the vector. For example, in the hexadecimal number output library routine (see chapter four), we find

```
WRCH((N&15)!TABLE
    '∅','1','2','3','4','5','6','7',
    '8','9','A','B','C','D','E','F')
```

which outputs the hexadecimal representation of the value stored in the bottom four bits of N.

Manifest constants are particularly well suited to describing data-structure layouts. Some consecutive words of store may represent a node in a data structure, with various words within the node serving different purposes (e.g. a chain pointer, a count, a value, an age). With suitable manifest constants we may write constructions such as

```
CURRENTITEM!AGE      CURRENTITEM!CHAINPOINTER
```

where CURRENTITEM points to the node. A popular fashion (noting that ! is commutative) is to write these in reverse order, reading the character ! as 'in'; e.g.

```
AGE!CURRENTITEM    reads as    'AGE in CURRENTITEM'
```

Remember that there is no runtime overhead incurred in using manifest constants, and that the extra typing effort is repaid many times in saving subsequent debugging and the efforts of others trying to understand your program.

3.2.1   Example: the compiler tree-structure

An example of the use of pointers to manipulate data structures other than arrays is the tree-structure representation of a program established by the BCPL compiler (see chapter six for more details). Each node in the tree consists of several consecutive words of store. The first word contains identifying information (represented in the program as a manifest constant), and the remaining words contain appropriate values or pointers to other nodes.

For example, the tree representing the namelist ABC, PQR, XYZ is shown in figure 3.2

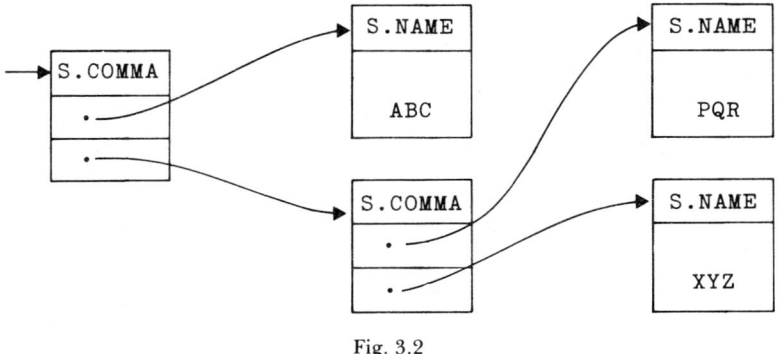

Fig. 3.2

The function to construct a namelist is

```
LET RNAMELIST() = VALOF
$( LET A = RNAME() // returns a pointer to a S.NAME node
   UNLESS SYMB = S.COMMA RESULTIS A
   NEXTSYMB()
   RESULTIS LIST3(S.COMMA, A, RNAMELIST())
$)
```

LIST3 is defined as

```
LET LIST3(X, Y, Z) = VALOF
$( LET P = NEWVEC(2)  // a function which allocates a vector
   P!Ø, P!1, P!2 := X, Y, Z
   RESULTIS P
$)
```

Details of how to allocate space (i.e. the implementation of NEWVEC) are discussed in chapters four and six.

3.2.2   Example: matrix storage

As a sophisticated example, we can establish the structure of a two-dimensional matrix within a vector. Assuming an M×N matrix, we can allocate the first M locations of a sufficiently large vector to contain pointers to the M individual rows. Each row has N elements, and successive rows are stored consecutively in the vector following the table of pointers. We assume that M and N have been declared as manifest constants. A vector of sufficient size is declared and initialised as follows:

```
LET V = VEC M*(N+1)-1
FOR I = Ø TO M-1 DO V!I := V + M + (N * I)
```

If M = 2 and N = 4, the matrix is represented diagrammatically as in figure 3.3.

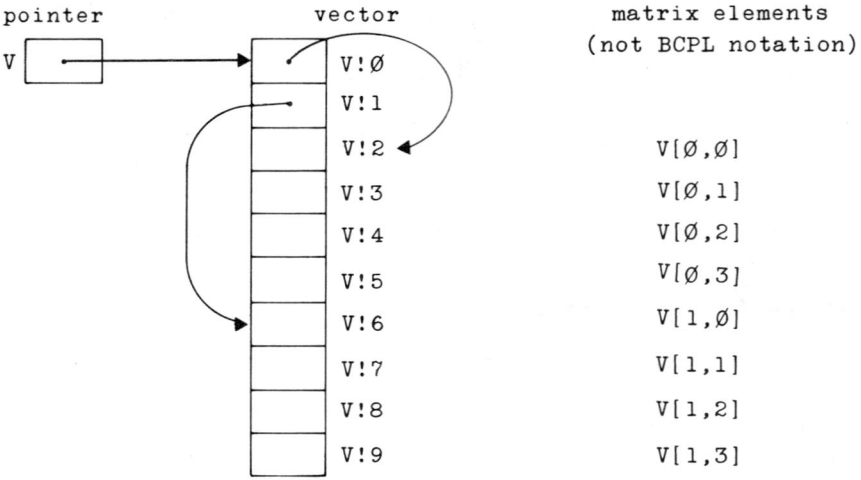

Fig. 3.3

To access the I, Jth element, we first access the Ith element of the vector V; this gives us a pointer to the Ith row. We then access the Jth element of this row, and so this element can be accessed by the expression V!I!J.

This exercise demonstrates two points:

(i) Multilevel use of pointers is straightforward. You can construct arbitrarily complicated data structures within a vector (and across several vectors if you take care), but both the establishment and manipulation of these data structures are your responsibility. With all but the simplest structures it is good practice to write procedures and functions to perform commonly used manipulations.

(ii) As a special case of (i), you can represent multi-dimensional matrices. If you wish, you can store sparse or triangular matrices efficiently.

3.3   Handling conceptual data types

Whenever you invent a new conceptual type that cannot be represented by a single BCPL value (e.g. a symbol table, or a bit string), then you should develop a set of routines and functions which perform all required operations on it. The internal representation of your new conceptual type, in terms of data structures, pointers, bit-packing and the use of other conceptual types, need only be known within this set of routines.

By way of example, you may well need to use a symbol table. You decide upon the operations required (e.g. does symbol S exist within the symbol table, insert symbol S with associated value T in the symbol table, remove symbol S, associate a new value with S, produce a list of symbols with value T) and the internal workings (use of vectors, pointers, hashcoding for table lookup etc.). The routines and functions may, in turn, call on other routines and functions which deal with the abstractions of 'symbol' and 'list'. The net effect is that users of the symbol table are neither interested in, nor care about, the internal workings of the symbol table, or of symbols themselves. A program change could be made (e.g. a new hashing function or table lookup technique employed) without any other routines being affected.

Further reading on this topic may be found in Parnas's paper on modular decomposition [9] and in the descriptions of Simula [3] and CLU [7] which both contain language constructions to support, in effect, data abstraction.

Exercise V

Design a multi-precision integer arithmetic package. Your package should include the procedures PLUS, MINUS, TIMES, DIVIDE, PRINT and READ, together with procedures to convert between single length and multiple length integers. Consider carefully various possible representations (e.g. making maximum use of all the bits in each word, as against storing values up to a convenient power of ten in each word). Hence, by implementing sufficient of your package, calculate and print the decimal value of $2^{2048} - 1$.

3.4   Procedure parameters

The BCPL procedure call uses the call-by-value technique for parameter passing. Thus, when you make a call such as F(X), it is the value of X that is passed into F and not its address and so there is no direct way to alter X from inside F. On the inside of the procedure, the values of the parameters at the moment of call are assigned to the corresponding formal parameters as declared in the procedure declaration. To all intents and purposes, the formal parameters of the procedure are simply local variables.

We discuss now what happens to pointers. Assume that we have a procedure P with one formal parameter A, i.e. P is declared by

```
LET P(A) BE . . .
```

Consider the case where V is declared (outside P) by

```
LET V = VEC 3Ø
```

The value passed to the procedure P by the call

```
P(V)
```

is the value held in the variable V which, assuming that no assignments have been made to it, is a BCPL pointer to the zeroth element of the vector. This value is copied into the formal parameter A, and thus the elements of the vector may be accessed from within P by writing

```
A!Ø, A!1, A!2, etc.
```

If we wish to change the contents of a dynamic variable declared outside a procedure, then we have to pass a pointer to it. This could be done either by storing the pointer in a static variable (a back door method), by passing the value of another variable which already holds its address (this is in effect what happens with vectors), or by using the ∂ construction to pass its address.

Thus to interchange the contents of two variables we could write a procedure

```
LET SWAP(PX,PY) BE
$(  //  PX and PY point to the two variables
    //  to be interchanged
    LET TEMP = !PX   //  value of X
    !PX := !PY       //  Y copied into X
    !PY := TEMP      //  and original X into Y
$)
```

and to call SWAP, we pass the addresses of the variables

```
SWAP(∂A, ∂B)
```

3.5 Recursion

All procedures in BCPL may be used *recursively*, i.e. every procedure may call itself (either directly or by calling other procedures which in turn call the original procedure). Every time a procedure is called, a new set of local variables (and formal parameters) is established. Of course you are not obliged to design recursive procedures, but sometimes a problem has a 'back-to-front' recursive solution. An example is a procedure to print decimal numbers. Such a procedure (let's call it PRINT) might be called to print, 1643, say. The easiest method of obtaining the digits is to split the number into two parts using the operators REM and /; i.e.

```
1643  REM 1Ø = 3
1643  / 1Ø = 164
```

We thus obtain the digit 3, which can easily be converted into a character code and printed. We then repeat the process on 164, and so on. Unfortunately, this produces the digits in the wrong order.

However, this difficulty can be averted neatly by using recursion. As before, the number is split into two parts, but this time the procedure is called recursively to print 164 before printing the character 3. The procedure will be called two more times recursively to print 16 and 1. On this final call, the number to be printed is less than 10, and so can be printed as a single digit, thus further recursion is not needed. The innermost call will print 1, and will then exit to the previous level of recursion, which will print 6, and so on. Our PRINT procedure thus becomes

```
LET PRINT(N) BE
$( IF N > 9 DO PRINT(N/1Ø)   // print all digits
                             // except the last one
   WRCH('Ø' + N REM 1Ø)      // print last digit
$)
```

Every time PRINT is called, a new copy is made of the value to be printed. On inner (recursive) calls, this will be 1/10 of the immediate outer value. Thus if we looked at all the program variables at the moment that WRCH was first called after PRINT had been asked to print the number 547, we would find three variables called N associated with the three recursive calls on PRINT. The innermost would contain 5, the next would contain 54, and the original would contain 547. Further reading on the topic of recursion may be found in Barron [2].

As a final point, tests on compiled BCPL programs have shown that dynamic variable allocation (the mechanism implementing recursion) is usually more efficient (with savings of up to 20% on program size, store usage and program speed) than static allocation, particularly on hardware with small-size addressing fields and few machine registers. This applies even if you do not take advantage of recursion. For this you have to pay the price of the very local nature of local variables. With good programming style this is no great hardship and, indeed, the restriction prevents some of the side-effects which are often the source of hard-to-find program bugs.

3.6   Scope rules: who knows about what

If you imagine a complete BCPL program module as being conceptually enclosed in a $($) pair, i.e. as the inner part of a block, then the scope rules can be easily explained.

    Identifiers declared at the head of a block can be used in the same and subsequent declarations and throughout the rest of the block, with the exception that procedure parameters, simple variables and vectors cannot be used inside embedded procedures. The following example illustrates this rule:

Scope (i.e. is accessible)

	P	X	G	Y	Q	R
LET P(X) BE						
$(GLOBAL $(G:1ØØ $)	+	+				
LET Y = X	+	+	+	+		
LET Q( ) BE	+		+			
$(						
R( )	+		+		+	+
$)						
AND R( ) BE	+		+		+	+
$(						
Q( )	+		+		+	+
$)						
. . .	+	+	+	+	+	+
$)						
. . .	+					

    The controlled variable in a for-command (e.g. the variable I in FOR I = 1 TO 5 DO . . .) may only be referenced from within the controlled command.

3.7   Other controls

BCPL recognises that there are occasions in which the need arises for greater flexibility in the construction of repetitive commands. Firstly, we consider termination. The test for termination is carried out either at the head or at the tail of the repetitive command. Sometimes it is easier to carry out a test for termination from within the body of the repetitive command. Often the body contains a branching construction (e.g. a switchon-command) in which some of the branches should lead to termination. The break-command provides a simple construction that meets this need.

    For example, the debug package (see chapter five) contains a routine that reads in a number in a given radix. In this we wish to read digits (including A, B, C, D, E

and F for hexadecimal numbers) until we meet a character not representing a digit
in the radix. The routine is as follows:

```
LET RDN(RADIX) = VALOF
$(1 LET A,SW = Ø, FALSE
    $( LET D = -1
       IF 'Ø'<=CH<='9' DO D := CH-'Ø'
       IF 'A'<=CH<='F' DO D := 1Ø+CH-'A'
       UNLESS Ø<=D<RADIX BREAK
       SW := TRUE
       A := A*RADIX + D
       CH := RDCH()    $) REPEAT
    UNLESS SW DO ERROR("BAD NUMBER")
    RESULTIS A    $)1
```

The first character is already in the global CH. The main part of the routine
iterates until a character not within the range of the radix is read. SW will be false if
no number is present, but is set TRUE if the loop repeats at least once.

The break-command says 'jump out of the smallest enclosing repetitive command'. It works inside the body of any of the repetitive commands FOR, WHILE,
UNTIL, REPEAT, REPEATWHILE, REPEATUNTIL. You should take care to
remember that only part of the repetitive command was executed when BREAK
was encountered.

There are other ways of exiting from the middle of a loop. For example, this
need is often coupled with the need to exit from an enclosing procedure. This can
be met by using RETURN or RESULTIS.

BCPL provides yet another control facility – the loop-command. This allows
you to skip the rest of the commands in the repetitive command, but remain inside
it. In the case of FOR, the controlled variable is incremented and, conditionally,
the repetitive command repeated. Within UNTIL, WHILE, REPEATUNTIL and
REPEATWHILE, the use of LOOP transfers control to the point at which the test is
made. For REPEAT, the repetitive command just starts again.

LOOP is used in situations where you discover early on in a repetitive command
that the rest of the command can be skipped and so the next thing to do is to test
whether to execute the command again or not.

3.8   Bit-operations

BCPL has several operators for logical bit-operations. For example

```
X := X & #377
```

forms the bitwise logical 'and' of X and the octal constant 377, effectively retaining only the last eight bits of X. The full set of operators is

```
<<      left shift
>>      right shift
¬       logical-not (bitwise inversion)
&       logical-and
|       logical-or
NEQV    logical-not-equivalence (exclusive-or)
EQV     equivalence
```

```
e.g. #42  |  #2Ø evaluates to #62
     #42<<3      evaluates to #24Ø
     #42>>2      evaluates to #1Ø
```

Care has to be taken with the BCPL precedence rules (see chapter eight). The precedence order of the logical operators is

> most binding <<, >> (but see chapter eight)
>
> ¬
>
> &
>
> |
>
> least binding EQV, NEQV

Thus

```
A + B >> C | D & E
```

is equivalent to

```
(( A + B ) >> C ) | ( D & E )
```

If you are simply joining conditionals together by using the logical operators, e.g. in

```
IF X>Y & A<=B THEN . . .
```

then brackets are not necessary. However, until you feel really confident about the BCPL precedence rules it is safest to use brackets liberally. Indeed, it is a good habit to use brackets, remembering that your program might be read (and altered) by someone less familiar with BCPL. Note the following typical case where the use of brackets is necessary:

```
IF ( A & #377 ) = 'P' DO  . . .
```

Without brackets, the compiler would read this as

```
IF A & (#377 = 'P') DO  . . .
```

As in this example, the operators &, |, ¬, EQV and NEQV are often used in BCPL to manipulate truth values. If the expression so formed is producing a truth value within the testing part of an IF, UNLESS, WHILE, etc., then evaluation is strictly left-to-right and evaluation ceases once the truth value is determined. For example, if B(X) is a function which produces a Boolean result, then it will never be called in the following test:

```
IF 1<2 | B(X) DO  . . .
```

Exercise VI

Write a BCPL function with one parameter which returns as result the number of bits set to 1 in the parameter.

3.9   Goto-commands and labels

BCPL does have goto-commands and labels. However, most of the time goto-commands are not needed. Your program can almost always be more clearly expressed by the other repetitive commands (FOR, WHILE etc.), by using IF and TEST constructs with compound commands and by using the ENDCASE, BREAK and LOOP control-transfer primitives.

A label declaration is written as an identifier followed by :. For most purposes it can be treated naively as in other programming languages, to identify a point in the program text. Strictly speaking, BCPL uses an indirect interpretation. The label identifier is associated with a static location (i.e. it can be treated as a static variable), which the compiler initialised to contain a BCPL value representing a point in the (compiled) program text. This value can thus be assigned to other variables, passed as a parameter (or indeed mutilated) like any other BCPL value. The construction

GOTO expression

means 'evaluate the expression, and transfer control to the point in the program represented by its value'. Usually, the expression takes the form of a variable declared by a label declaration. Note that the static variable itself can be assigned to, which, with careful use, provides a dynamic jump facility (which should be annotated very carefully), or, with careless use, provides ready chaos.

3.10   Typeless names – or context type determination

You can use BCPL in the manner described in the previous chapter, using different variables for the different objects of your program without thinking too much what the compiler makes of it all. However, there are some consequences of the BCPL approach, described in chapter one, which you can use (or abuse) once you become more fluent in the language. If you find that you cannot accept the BCPL philosophy about type, then you should probably use a systems-programming language with compile-time type checking, such as C or Pascal.

When you declare an identifier in BCPL, you are stating its name, how it is to be stored, and possibly indicating an initial value. You do not say how you intend to use it. The compiler may restrict your use of an identifier by various scope rules, but that is a consequence of the implementation storage strategy.

The value of an identifier is always representable as a pattern of bits (how many bits depends upon the implementation). The interpretation to be placed on the bit-pattern in no way depends upon how the identifier was declared, but only on how it is used in your program, i.e. what operators, functions etc. you apply to it.

The corollary to this is that you can apply any operator (other than @) to absolutely any named object in your BCPL program. This gives you at one and the same time great freedom and great responsibility.

3.11   Procedures as values

BCPL has been carefully designed so that it is possible to represent a procedure by a simple BCPL value, which we will call the *procedure value*. In many implementations this is the procedure's entry address. The translated procedure is stored in a sequence of locations, which start at a known address. The procedure value is placed in a variable bearing the name of the procedure. In other words, the variable can be thought of as containing the start address of the procedure. If the name of the procedure coincides with that of a global variable then this variable is used to store the procedure value, otherwise a new static variable (see section 3.12 for details of static variables) is used. For example,

```
GLOBAL $( START:1 $)
LET START( ) BE
   $(      . . .        $)
```

causes global variable number 1 to be initialised to the procedure value of START.

This is the only way of initialising global variables prior to executing the program.

Procedure values can be assigned to ordinary variables, as in the following extract from the library routine WRITEF (described in chapter four):

```
$(3 LET F, ARG, N = Ø, T!Ø, Ø
    P := P + 1
    $( LET CH = GETBYTE(FORMAT, P)
       SWITCHON CH INTO
       $( . . .
          CASE 'S': F := WRITES; GOTO L
          CASE 'C': F := WRCH; GOTO L
          . . .
       $)
       . . .
    L: F(ARG, N); . . .
```

The variable F is set to contain the procedure value for one of several output procedures, depending upon the control character in CH. The appropriate procedure is subsequently called to generate the desired output.

A further consequence is that a procedure may be passed as a parameter to another procedure, or returned as the result of a function call.

The general format of a procedure call is

expression(parameters)

Usually we use the declared procedure name as the expression, but there is nothing to prevent us from writing an arbitrarily complicated expression. The expression must be enclosed in brackets in all but the simple cases, as a procedure call takes precedence over all other operators.

3.11.1 *Example: OS6 stream structure*

As an example, we describe the use of procedure values in the stream structure of OS6, which is an operating system written in BCPL by Stoy and Strachey [12]. In OS6, the programmer can manipulate streams of input and output. The function call NEXT(S) can be applied to any input stream S, and produces the next character. Similarly OUT(T,X) outputs the character X to the output stream T. Some streams are bi-directional.

All the relevant information concerning a particular stream S is stored in a vector (to which S points). The first few items in this vector are procedure values. The vector takes the form shown in figure 3.4,

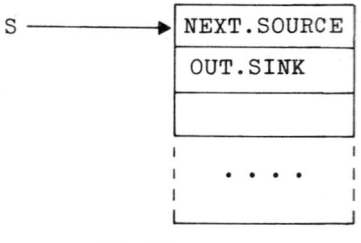

Fig. 3.4

where NEXT.SOURCE is the function which implements NEXT for S (it may well be a different function for different streams) etc. Stream-creating functions themselves take the form

```
LET INPUTFROMTTY = VALOF
$(  LET V = NEWVEC(5)     // claiming a vector from a
                          // freestore package
    V!Ø := NEXTTTY        // the procedure value for NEXTTTY
    V!1 := STREAMERROR     // for an input stream
    .  .  .
    RESULTIS V
$)
```

Thus the procedure value held in the zeroth element of S represents the function which implements NEXT for stream S. NEXT is thus defined as

```
LET NEXT(S) = (S!Ø)(S)
```

Similarly, OUT is defined as

```
LET OUT(S, X) BE (S!1)(S, X)
```

OS6 allows streams with special properties (e.g. removing surplus layout characters, or using translation tables) to be established using the system-provided streams. The reader is referred to Stoy and Strachey [13, 14] for further details of this interesting operating system.

3.12   Static variables

The global vector is an example of permanently allocated storage in BCPL, as opposed to the temporarily allocated storage of local variables. It is primarily designed for linking independently compiled modules, but when permanently allocated storage is required within a single module then the static declaration is to be preferred. This introduces the names and initial values of the static variables. Static variables are initialised before the program starts execution. An example of the use of a static variable is

```
LET  NEXTID( ) = VALOF
             // generates a sequence of integer identifiers
$( STATIC  $( NUMBER = Ø  $)
    NUMBER := NUMBER + 1
    RESULTIS NUMBER      //delivers 1 on first entry
                         //          2 on second entry, etc.
$)
```

3.13 Separate compilation facilities

You should familiarise yourself with the facilities in BCPL for separate compilation of physical source modules (some installations refer to these as segments). If any source BCPL program or module occupies more than four or five pages of lineprinter listing, then it should be considered for splitting into separate pieces. An even better approach is to anticipate this; it is easy to forget how rapidly a program can grow. When you first design a program, design in separate compilation from the beginning (which is also a good programming discipline) even if the modules are only half a page long. Put the global and manifest declarations required throughout the program into a separate file and use GET at the head of each module. Declarations global to several routines but local to a module, however, should not be allowed to find their way into this file.

The global vector forms the basis of the independent compilation facilities of BCPL. In contrast to local variables, if you declare a procedure with the same name as a global variable, then this global variable becomes associated with the procedure by the compiler setting it to contain the procedure value (typically the address of the procedure in the computer's program memory). The global variable should therefore not be used for anything else. So if we declare a procedure called COUNTER somewhere in the program after declaring a global variable COUNTER, then this procedure is available to all parts of the program. We can, in fact, divide our program into two pieces (which we will call modules) which can be compiled separately. Both modules start with the same global declarations, and thus can access the same global variables. However, only one module contains the procedure to be associated with COUNTER; i.e. Module A (compiled on Tuesday):

```
GET "LIBHDR"
GLOBAL $(  NUMBER:  1ØØ;  COUNTER:1Ø1  $)
LET START( ) BE
$(  .  .  .
    NUMBER := 543
    COUNTER( )              //  call the global procedure
    .  .  .
$)
```

Module B (compiled on Wednesday):

```
GLOBAL $( NUMBER:1ØØ;  COUNTER:1Ø1  $)
LET COUNTER( ) BE
$(  .  .  .
    FOR I = 1 TO NUMBER DO   // using the global variable
    .  .  .
$)
```

We could then load the two modules side-by-side and run the complete program on Thursday.

Exercises VII

1. Write a program to generate a random binary tree of 100 nodes, each containing a random integer in the range 0 to 5.

2. Write a program to make a copy of the tree produced by 1 above in such a way that identical branches of the tree share the same memory. Print the number of distinct nodes used in this copy.

3. Write a program to count the number of ways in which eight queens can be laid out on a chess board in such a way that no queen is on the same row, column or diagonal as any other.

4

The library, language extensions, and machine independence

Most BCPL implementations comprise a set of basic procedures (some written in the local assembly language), together with a standard library of procedures written in BCPL. The basic procedures provide the means of accessing the operating-system functions and machine-level facilities without the programmer having to depart from BCPL.

4.1   Basic input and output procedures

Available to the program are a set of input and a set of output streams. The routine SELECTINPUT is used to select an input stream, from which all subsequent input will be taken until the next call of SELECTINPUT. Similarly SELECTOUTPUT is used to select an output stream, to which all subsequent output will be sent until the next call of SELECTOUTPUT. The argument of SELECTINPUT or SELECTOUTPUT is a BCPL value which represents a stream in some implementation-dependent way. On some implementations, integers are used; however, it is more usual for a stream to be represented by a pointer to a data control block containing all the information relevant to the stream.

In many implementations, the association between these values and the physical input/output devices, files etc. can be controlled dynamically. To gain access to these facilities, procedures with names such as FINDINPUT, FINDOUTPUT and FINDFILE are provided as appropriate. On initial entry to a BCPL program, a default selection of an input and an output stream will usually have been made by the system, and so it is often not necessary to invoke any of these procedures in simple programs.

Single-character input and output is provided by RDCH, the function which reads a character, and WRCH, the routine to output a character. If RDCH is called when the currently selected input is exhausted, it yields the conventional value ENDSTREAMCH. This is a manifest constant whose value is usually −1, to differentiate it from any valid character. Streams can be closed by using the routines ENDREAD and ENDWRITE whose exact effects are implementation dependent.

4.2   *Input and output library facilities*

The basic procedures just described provide a level of machine independence on which a standardised BCPL library is constructed. The most satisfactory way of specifying the library is by describing its implementation in terms of these basic procedures. This also demonstrates the typical ways in which they are used.

4.2.1   *Numbers*

```
LET WRITED(N,D) BE
$(1  LET T = VEC 2Ø
     AND I, K = Ø, -N
     IF N<Ø DO D, K := D-1, N
     T!I, K, I := -(K REM 1Ø), K/1Ø, I+1 REPEATUNTIL K=Ø
     FOR J = I+1 TO D DO WRCH('*S')
     IF N<Ø DO WRCH('-')
     FOR J = I-1 TO Ø BY -1 DO WRCH(T!J+'Ø')   $)1
```

This routine outputs N as a signed decimal integer, occupying at least D printing positions. The digits are stored in reverse order in the vector T, and the routine works with negative values to overcome the problem of negating the largest negative number in 2's complement representation. Note that this routine relies upon the 'correct' operation of REM with a negative left operand (strictly speaking not defined in BCPL), and that consecutive numerical representation of digits in the character code is assumed.

The routine to output a number in the minimum number of printing positions is simply

```
LET WRITEN(N) BE WRITED(N, Ø)
```

The following function reads in a decimal number (possibly preceded by + or −), ignoring leading spaces, tabs and newlines:

```
LET READN() = VALOF
$(1  LET SUM = Ø
     AND NEG = FALSE
     AND CH = Ø
     CH := RDCH() REPEATWHILE CH='*S' |
                              CH='*T' |
                              CH='*N'
```

```
SWITCHON CH INTO
$(  CASE '-':    NEG := TRUE
    CASE '+':    CH := RDCH()    $)
WHILE 'Ø'<=CH<='9' DO
            $(  SUM := 1Ø*SUM + CH - 'Ø'
                CH := RDCH()        $)
IF NEG THEN SUM := -SUM
TERMINATOR := CH
RESULTIS SUM        $)1
```

Notice that, on some implementations using 2's complement representation of integers, this function will fail to yield the correct value for the largest negative integer.

The next routine provides octal output:

```
LET WRITEOCT(N, D) BE
   $( IF D>1 DO WRITEOCT(N>>3, D-1)
      WRCH((N&7) + 'Ø')    $)
```

If this routine is called, for example, by WRITEOCT(#173, 3) then it calls itself recursively with WRITEOCT(#17,2) and recurses again with WRITEOCT(#1,1). In this deepest level of recursion, the parameter D is set to 1, and so the routine WRCH is called (for the first time) to output the character corresponding to the bottom three bits of N ('1'). On exit to the middle level of recursion, N will contain 17, and so WRCH is called to output the character '7'. Finally WRCH is called from the outermost level to output the character '3'. Thus the net effect of the original call is to write out the characters '1', '7' and '3' in that order.

A similar routine provides hexadecimal output:

```
LET WRITEHEX(N, D) BE
$( IF D>1 DO WRITEHEX(N>>4, D-1)
   WRCH((N&15)!TABLE 'Ø','1','2','3','4','5','6','7',
                     '8','9','A','B','C','D','E','F' )    $)
```

4.2.2 Strings

Exactly how BCPL strings are stored depends, amongst other things, upon the implementation word size. This dependency is concealed within the string-access procedures GETBYTE and PUTBYTE. The call

GETBYTE(S, I)

obtains the Ith byte of the string S. By convention, byte 0 contains the number of characters in the string, which are stored consecutively from byte 1. The call

```
PUTBYTE(S, I, C)
```

sets the Ith byte of the string S to contain the character C.

String output is implemented by WRITES defined as follows:

```
LET WRITES(S) BE
    FOR I = 1 TO GETBYTE(S,Ø) DO WRCH(GETBYTE(S,I))
```

GETBYTE(S,Ø) gives the number of characters in the string, which are then accessed by GETBYTE(S,I). Note that, while the number of bytes per word is implementation dependent, this is of no interest to the user of GETBYTE.

The following routine unpacks a string into a vector:

```
LET UNPACKSTRING(S, V) BE
    FOR I = Ø TO GETBYTE(S, Ø) DO V!I := GETBYTE(S, I)
```

Note that a vector of sufficient size has to be established before this routine is called. The function PACKSTRING performs the inverse operation using PUTBYTE:

```
LET PACKSTRING(V, S) = VALOF
$( LET N = V!Ø & #XFF
   LET SIZE = N/BYTESPERWORD
   S!SIZE := Ø
   FOR I = Ø TO N DO PUTBYTE(S, I, V!I)
   RESULTIS SIZE
$)
```

Note that the result of PACKSTRING is the subscript of the highest element of S used.

4.2.3   *Formatted output*

The routine WRITEF provides approximately the facilities of the Fortran WRITE statement. BCPL allows procedures to take a variable number of parameters, with no predisposition as to type, and so WRITEF is implemented as a library routine, and not as a statement of the language.

Its first parameter is a string, which contains substitution specifications each introduced by % followed by details of the printing style. Successive parameters of the call provide successive values to be substituted. The number of parameters required depends upon the format string. A typical call of WRITEF is

```
WRITEF("Break No %N at %X4*N", BREAKNO, A)
```

The %N instructs WRITEF to substitute the value of BREAKNO, printed as a decimal integer, and %X4 the value of A, printed as a four-digit hexadecimal number. This call would produce, typically,

```
Break No 5 at Ø3F8
```

We now give the text of WRITEF:

```
LET WRITEF(FORMAT, A, B, C, D, E, F, G, H, I, J, K) BE
$(1 LET T = ∂A

    FOR P = 1 TO GETBYTE(FORMAT, Ø) DO
    $(2 LET K = GETBYTE(FORMAT, P)

        TEST K = '%'

        THEN $(3 LET F, ARG, N = Ø, !T, Ø
                 P := P + 1
              $( LET CH = GETBYTE(FORMAT, P)
                 SWITCHON CH INTO
                 $( DEFAULT: WRCH(CH):        ENDCASE
                    CASE 'S': F := WRITES;   GOTO L
                    CASE 'C': F := WRCH;     GOTO L
                    CASE 'O': F := WRITEOCT; GOTO M
                    CASE 'X': F := WRITEHEX; GOTO M
                    CASE 'I': F := WRITED;   GOTO M
                    CASE 'N': F := WRITED;   GOTO L  $)

              M: P := P + 1
                 CH:= GETBYTE(FORMAT), P)
                 N := 'Ø'<=CH<='9' -> CH-'Ø',
                                      1Ø+CH-'A'

              L: F(ARG, N); T := T + 1  $)3

        ELSE WRCH(K)    $)2 $)1
```

T holds the pointer to the store location containing the next parameter to be substituted in the format, thus !T produces the corresponding value. Incrementing T advances it to point to the adjacent parameter. The variable F is used to hold the procedure value of the routine to be called to print the value in the specified format. Note that using a procedure name without brackets produces the corresponding procedure value, and does not invoke it.

BCPL does not require the number of actual parameters in a procedure call to equal the number of formal parameters in its definition. Parameters in excess of the number specified in the definition are lost. Hence this definition of WRITEF is only valid for calls having up to twelve parameters. Notice also that the call F(ARG, N) is valid when F is a monadic routine (such as WRITES) as the value of N is superfluous in this case.

4.3   Miscellaneous

Often included among the set of basic procedures is the function MULDIV(X, Y, Z). This evaluates (X * Y) / Z without overflow, providing that the correct result can be stored within the single word length of the implementation. It does this by dividing Z into the double-length product of X and Y. This function is especially useful in short word length implementations.

The following completes the main part of the BCPL library:

```
LET RANDOM(N) = 2147001325*N + 715136305
```

This is a congruential pseudo-random number generator. It has the property that the bottom n digits go through all 2^n possibilities in 2^n iterations. Note that, in particular, the result is alternately even and odd. The definition given above is for 32-bit implementations, and the calculation is assumed to be performed modulo 2^{32}. The right-hand bits of the two constants should be used as appropriate for shorter word length implementations. A typical use of RANDOM is

```
LET RANDNO()  = VALOF
   $( STATIC $( SEED = 0  $)
      SEED := RANDOM(SEED)
      RESULTIS (SEED>>7) & #77  $)
```

Notice that this function will produce exactly the same sequence on a 16-bit machine as on a 32-bit machine if the constants are truncated to 16 bits.

4.4   LEVEL and LONGJUMP

These two routines provide between them the means of transferring control across several layers of procedure invocation. We recall that the parameters, the dynamic variables and vectors of BCPL procedures are stored using a stack mechanism. Each procedure call results in a new stack frame being allocated to hold the dynamic variables etc. of this invocation of the called procedure. A procedure may obtain a BCPL value representing its stack frame by calling LEVEL( ). This value may then be stored, say, in a global variable for later reference to the stack frame.

We recall also that a label in BCPL is, in effect, a static or global variable which is initialised to a value representing the point in the program at which it is declared. Assume that we have written a procedure P, in which we declare a label L. Within P it is sensible to use the command GOTO L to transfer control to L. However, once control has passed to another procedure (Q say) the current stack frame will be that of an invocation of Q. Thus use of GOTO L within Q will result in a transfer of control into the program of P, but using Q's stack frame, leading to undefined and probably catastrophic effects. By contrast, on the normal completion of the body of Q, execution will resume at the point in P just after the call of Q with P's stack frame restored appropriately. In some (rare) circumstances (e.g. error handling), this is inconvenient, particularly if Q is reached only via several other procedures or if the point in P to which we wish to return is not where we left it. The solution is to memorise the stack frame of P (say, in the global P.STACKFRAME) and to instruct explicitly the BCPL runtime system to reinstate it on jumping to L. The routine LONGJUMP is provided for this purpose, and may be called thus:

```
LONGJUMP(P.STACKFRAME, L)
```

To illustrate a typical use of this facility, we refer to the debug package, described in chapter five. This contains, at the outermost level, the declaration of two static variables REC.P and REC.L. The main steering routine (DEBUG) is structured as follows:

```
    LET DEBUG( ) = VALOF
    $(1 . . .        //    declarations
        REC.P, REC.L := LEVEL( ), NXT
        . . .
NXT:  CH := RDCH( )
 SW:  SWITCHON CH INTO
      $( DEFAULT:  ERROR("BAD COMMAND %C", CH)
          . . .
      $)
    $)1
```

Then come other procedures, which are called from DEBUG under appropriate circumstances, which also contain calls of the error routine, for example:

ERROR("BAD NUMBER"). Finally, the error routine is defined as:

```
AND ERROR(S, A) BE
$(1 NEWLINE()
    WRITEF(S, A)
    NEWLINE()
    UNTIL CH='*N' DO CH := RDCH()
    LONGJUMP(REC.P, REC.L)    $)1
```

   Thus, on encountering an error, whether simply an unknown command detected in DEBUG, or a more subtle error detected in an inner procedure, an appropriate error message is output, the remainder of the current line is ignored, and control is transferred back into DEBUG to read the next command. A similar, but more sophisticated, example of the use of LEVEL and LONGJUMP will be found in the BCPL syntax analyser (chapter six).

4.5   APTOVEC

The BCPL method of declaring vectors is by using the let-declaration, e.g.

```
LET V = VEC 25
```

The size of the vector (in this example 26 words are allocated contiguously) must be specified at compile-time. This allows the compiler to calculate the exact size of the stack frame required for the enclosing procedure. Programmers are thereby constrained to ensure that the vectors will always be big enough to cover all requirements, even though this may mean wasting space in a majority of circumstances. To alleviate this difficulty when it is perceived as being serious, many implementations provide a facility which creates a vector whose size may be determined dynamically. This facility is provided by the function APTOVEC, whose definition is as follows:

```
LET APTOVEC(F, N) = VALOF
   $( LET V = VEC N   //    illegal in BCPL
      RESULTIS F(V, N)  $)
```

   APTOVEC is normally implemented in assembly language, since dynamic vector allocation is not permitted in BCPL. It will typically allocate space for the vector V on the stack just below the stack frame for the call of F. Thus on exit from F, via APTOVEC, to the calling procedure, the vector will be deallocated automatically. It can be used as follows:

```
LET START( ) BE
   $(  LET N = READN( )
       APTOVEC(MAINPROG, N)    $)

AND MAINPROG(V, N) BE .  .  .
```

4.6   Freestore management

Whilst the ability to choose dynamically the vector size alleviates some space-management problems, there are circumstances where the allocation of space bears no relationship with the flow of control through the procedure structure of a program. Under these circumstances the programmer has to be responsible for both the allocation and the deallocation of space. The following procedures can be used to provide such a facility in the form of a simple freestore-management system. This system uses a first-fit algorithm for allocating blocks of variable size. It coalesces adjacent free blocks and, although it is not particularly efficient, the procedures are compact.

In an outer block, the programmer declares a vector of suitable size and calls INITBLKLIST, e.g.

```
LET START( ) BE
$(  LET FREESTOREVEC = VEC FSVSIZE
    INITBLKLIST(FREESTOREVEC, FSVSIZE)
    .  .  .
```

This hands over the vector to the freestore-management system. In this system, FSVSIZE must be even. An allocation of space from this area may be made by calling the function GETBLK, e.g.

```
V := GETBLK(X+Y)
```

which returns a pointer to the allocated space. In this particular package, the first word of each block supplied is reserved for the package's use, but the remainder may be treated as an ordinary vector. When the space is no longer required, it is returned with the call

```
FREEBLK(V)
```

The package is defined for a 16-bit machine as follows:

```
GET "LIBHDR"

GLOBAL $(
BLKLIST:1ØØ; GETBLK:1Ø1; FREEBLK:1Ø2; INITBLKLIST:1Ø3
$)

MANIFEST $(
SIZEBITS=#XFFFE; FREEBIT=1
$)

LET INITBLKLIST(V,N) BE
    BLKLIST, V!Ø, V!N := V, N+FREEBIT, Ø

LET GETBLK(N) = VALOF  // N is the size of the required block
$(1 LET P, Q = Ø, BLKLIST

    N := (N+1) & SIZEBITS  // round up to next multiple of 2

    $( P := Q
       WHILE (!P&FREEBIT)=Ø DO // chain through used blocks
         TEST !P = Ø THEN RESULTIS Ø // end of store reached
                   ELSE P := P + !P
       Q := P  // chain to end of this free area
         UNTIL (!Q&FREEBIT)=Ø DO Q := Q + !Q - FREEBIT
    $) REPEATUNTIL Q-P> =N // until large enough block found
    UNLESS P+N=Q DO  // split block unless exact fit
            P!N := Q-P-N+FREEBIT
    !P := N
    RESULTIS P
$)1


LET FREEBLK(P) BE !P := !P | FREEBIT
```

Before allocating a block, the package makes sure that its size is a multiple of 2 (by rounding up). The first word is set to contain the size of the block. Thus all allocated blocks have the least significant bit set to zero. This bit is set to 1 (FREEBIT) when the space is returned. To find a free block of sufficient size, the package skips over the allocated blocks until a free block is found. The following free blocks are coalesced and the amalgamated block tested to see if it is of sufficient size. If not the process is repeated. If so then it is subdivided (if necessary) into the allocated block and a free block. If no large enough block is found GETBLK returns zero.

4.7 The floating-point extension

Some implementations contain extensions to support floating-point arithmetic. A floating-point constant may have one of the following forms:

$i.j\text{E}k$
$i.j$
$i\text{E}k$

where i and j are unsigned integers and k is a (possibly signed) integer. The value is represented on the IBM 370 as a 32-bit floating-point number.

The arithemtic and relational operators for floating-point quantities are as follows:

```
#*   #/
#+   #-
#=   #¬=   #<=   #>=   #<   #>
```

They have the same precedence as the corresponding integer operations. There are, also, two monadic functions FIX(X) and FLOAT(X) for conversions between integers and floating-point numbers. A common pitfall is to write -3.1 when #-3.1 is intended.

4.8 The field-selector extension

Some implementations support the field-selector extension. Field selectors allow quantities smaller than a whole word to be accessed with reasonable convenience and efficiency. A selector is applied to a pointer using the operator OF (or : :). It has three components: the size, the shift and the offset. The size is the number of bits in the field, the shift is the number of bits between the right-most bit of the field and the right-hand end of the word containing it, and the offset is the position of the word containing the field relative to the pointer. By convention, a size of zero specifies that the field extends to the left-hand end of the word.

The precedence of OF is the same as that of the subscription operator (!), but its left operand (the *selector*) must be a constant-expression. A convenient way to specify a selector is to use the operator SLCT whose syntax is as follows:

```
<constant expression> ::=   SLCT <size>:<shift>:<offset> |
                            SLCT <size>:<shift> |
                            SLCT <size>
```

where <size>, <shift> and <offset> are constant-expressions. Unless explicitly specified, the shift and offset are assumed zero by default. Selectors are best defined using manifest declarations.

A selector may be used on the left-hand side of an assignment and in any other context where an expression may be used, except as the operand of ə. In the assignment

```
F OF P := E
```

the appropriate number of bits from the right-hand end of E are assigned to the specified field. When

```
F OF P
```

is evaluated in any other context, the specified field is extracted and shifted so as to appear at the right-hand end of the result.

On some implementations, fields corresponding to half-words, bytes and individual bits are treated efficiently.

4.9   The infixed byte operator

The byte handling library procedures GETBYTE and PUTBYTE have been found to be so useful that many BCPL implementations have an infixed operator that provides the same facility. The preferred extension uses the operator % giving it identical precedence to the indirection operator ! . Its use on the left-hand side of an assignment invokes PUTBYTE. For example,

```
S%I := CH
```

is equivalent to

```
PUTBYTE(S, I, CH)
```

In other contexts, S%I is equivalent to GETBYTE(S,I).

4.10   Techniques for machine independence and portability

Machine independence is easy to achieve in BCPL for the main body of an algorithm or program provided that you adopt a simple and clear programming style. However, designing for portability does require some care:

(*a*) Put all machine-dependent material in one module. This includes all calls on standard library procedures, initialisation code where this depends upon an external interface (e.g. how options are specified on entry to the program), any procedures that will need adapting to use a different word size (alternative versions, or readily changed manifest constants should be provided). Keep the external (system-dependent) interface as simple and as flexible as possible. Note that many computer systems do not permit character-by-character interaction on on-line terminals.

(*b*) Carefully avoid code which makes use of representation, particularly of numbers and of strings. For example, right shift may divide by two on your installation, but may not on another.

(*c*) Differing word sizes can cause problems. Carefully document all places in your program where arithmetic range limitations may apply (e.g. it may be in your program that the maximum value of a parameter is the square root of the maximum number that can be held in a machine word). Remember that more vector space will be needed to pack a character string on a small word size machine than on a large one. The manifest constant **BYTESPERWORD** should be used in the appropriate vector declarations. A string of **N** characters packs into 1 + **N/BYTESPERWORD** cells.

(*d*) Beware of problems due to differing character sets. Write programs that still work even when all lower-case characters are converted to upper-case. Make no assumptions about the number of bits in a character. This is usually 8, and consequently the longest string is defined to be 255 characters. Nevertheless, keep strings short. Always use character quotes and escapes; never write the installation-dependent value of a character.

5

Debugging and error handling

Ensuring that a program performs as intended is a problem in any programming system. Inevitably, the newcomer to BCPL will also be caught unawares by differences of BCPL from his accustomed programming language. In this chapter, we first examine some of the compiler-detected errors, and then discuss the techniques available to aid fault detection in programs that compile but do not work correctly. We conclude with a list of common mistakes as an aid to trouble-shooting.

5.1 Syntax errors

Many syntax errors can be easily located with the help of the compiler's error messages. However, it sometimes happens that slips in BCPL programs cannot be determined as being erroneous until compilation has proceeded for some distance. As part of the syntax error reporting, the last-read sixty-four characters of the program are printed, nevertheless error messages produced at the moment when the error is detected are somewhat imprecise, as the fault could well have occurred well prior to the current symbol. We discuss some of the syntactic slips which are particularly prone to causing this effect.

5.1.1 Missing colon in :=

The compiler reads, for example, A = B (instead of A := B) as the start of an expression. Several commands start with expressions and the error is often not detected until one or two lines further on, for example if B is a large valof-expression. The latest line read, though doubtless syntactically perfect, will be displayed as (probably) containing the error. Thus it is always advisable to look back in your program for a malformed command.

5.1.2 Extra semicolons

A semicolon may be used to separate one command from the next. This is in contrast to some other languages where it is used as a terminator. Two consecutive semicolons is erroneous, and a common error is to put one before the closing $) of a compound command or block. These two errors cause the message 'ERROR IN COMMAND' to be printed. In fact you hardly ever need to use semicolons. In particular, a semicolon may always be omitted if it is the last symbol of a line, and it may be omitted in most other contexts.

5.1.3 THEN *or* DO *needed*

DO is a synonym of THEN, and, like the semicolon, may be omitted except where needed to remove local ambiguity. An example of the type of construction where it is necessary is

```
IF B THEN !P := Ø
```

It is wise to omit THEN only if it occurs immediately before a command keyword.

5.1.4 *Mismatched section brackets*

This can cause problems in all stages of compiling and running a program. The solution is to lay out your program neatly to reflect the nesting structure. Beware of the problems that the occasional use of section bracket tags can bring. The closing tagged bracket inserts extra closing brackets to close off any inner blocks or compound commands – thus preventing the compiler from detecting a previously omitted $). When a program with this error is run, the user is often baffled because a large portion of his program is not obeyed. As an exercise, consider the effect of omitting the $) on line 480 of the syntax analyser (described on page 102 in chapter six). You should either use tagged section brackets very liberally (no 'untagged' compound command or block more than, say, three lines long) or not use them at all.

5.1.5 *Inadvertent tagging*

A frequent fault amongst newcomers to BCPL is to omit the necessary space between an opening section bracket and the first declaration or·command, e.g.

```
writing     $(LET A = Ø
instead of  $( LET A = Ø
```

which misleadingly produces the message 'ERROR IN COMMAND'. A good habit is to put each section bracket on a line by itself; this also serves to emphasise the block nesting structure of the program.

5.1.6   String problems

In older versions of the BCPL compiler, the misuse of string quotes would cause it
to generate wild diagnostics, as most of the program would be swallowed up as
belonging to some string, whilst the strings themselves would not form good
BCPL syntax. Remember that to include an asterisk in a string requires you to type
**, and a double quotes character requires * ". In recent versions, the effect is less
dramatic, as unescaped newline is no longer permitted in strings.

5.2   Semantic errors

The semantic errors are detected in a compiler pass after the syntax analysis has
been completed, and the original source text is no longer available for pinpointing
errors. However, in practice, programs tend to have few compiler detected
semantic errors, and those that do occur tend to be concerned with the misuse of
variables. The name of the offending variable is usually sufficient information for
the programmer. However, there is one error in this class which tends to trip up
the programmer used to other block-structured languages:

DYNAMIC FREE VARIABLE USED

   Every BCPL programmer meets this at least once (usually several times) during
his apprenticeship. Dynamic variables (e.g. simple variables and vectors declared
using **LET**) can be used in inner blocks, but they cannot be used in procedures
embedded in the block.
   The reason for this follows from an aim of BCPL to eliminate hidden overheads. Dynamic variables are stored using a stack mechanism. Each activation of a
procedure is allocated a stack frame, and a runtime pointer is maintained to the
current stack frame. By imposing this restriction, the compiler is able to reference
all dynamic variables as offsets from this pointer (which will usually be stored in a
suitable machine index register), thus employing simple and efficient code.
Furthermore, recursion is implemented without any additional complication.
   This restriction only applies to dynamic variables, so you can use functions and
procedures (which also are declared using **LET**), globals, labels and static variables
that are declared outside the current procedure. If you still have problems, then
re-read sections 2.12 and 2.14. Most systems programmers admit that this is a
reasonable restriction once they understand the implementation issues involved.

5.3   Runtime error handling

The BCPL philosophy of giving runtime freedom to the programmer allows him
to write efficient and compact programs. However, the careless programmer who

is accustomed to relying on the implementation to check the meaningfulness of his program will meet many difficulties with BCPL. This can be regarded as a hidden blessing, as it imposes the need for a careful stylistic approach to the design of BCPL programs. We discuss first the considerations that should be given to error handling, and in the later sections of this chapter we describe how the same runtime freedom can be exploited to provide powerful yet compact program debugging tools.

Error handling should be considered at an early stage in the design of a program. The phrase may be taken to include both detection and recovery. There is no built-in checking of array bounds etc. in BCPL, so explicit error checking should be considered. The procedures that maintain data structures should incorporate a certain degree of error checking (e.g. values, address offsets within range etc.). To effect error recovery, they should maintain consistency when an error is detected (e.g. by substituting null or harmless values, and by ensuring that data structures are not left only half filled etc.). Well-defined error indications should be designed into the procedure interfaces, so that an inner procedure which is unable to conceal an error can pass up responsibility for containment to the calling procedure.

By designing in a substantial degree of error checking, you will have made considerable progress towards providing yourself (and anyone else who may use or modify your program) with a purpose-built debugging tool. A faulty value, generated by an erroneous procedure, could well be trapped soon afterwards by the incorporated redundancy before too much damage occurs obscuring the original fault.

5.4 BACKTRACE, MAPSTORE, *and* ABORT

Many BCPL implementations provide a number of post-mortem facilities. BACKTRACE is a procedure that inspects the BCPL stack, printing out part of the contents of each stack frame. Setting suitable compiler options allows BACKTRACE to display the print name of each active procedure. The output thus records the most recent procedure call at each nested level, together with its arguments and first few dynamic variables.

MAPSTORE prints out the contents of the global vector, followed by a map of the program area consisting of the names and addresses in store of separately compiled modules, the start of procedures, and execution counts. The level of detail produced by MAPSTORE is controlled through compiler options. Very detailed information is produced by MAPSTORE when used in conjunction with the profile option (see below).

The BACKTRACE and MAPSTORE procedures provide examples of how the addressing flexibility of BCPL can be harnessed to good effect. They are both extremely machine dependent, since BACKTRACE makes use of detailed knowledge of the runtime stack, whilst MAPSTORE searches the compiled program for specific machine instructions. Despite this, the overall organisation of these procedures is similar in most implementations.

A procedure called ABORT completes the set of post-mortem procedures. ABORT can be called from within a program or via an appropriate operating system facility (such as program store trap). We conclude this section with the text of this post-mortem package as implemented on the ModComp II machine (a 16-bit word-addressed minicomputer).

```
GET "LIBHDR"

MANIFEST $( ENTRYWORD1 =#XF813
            ENTRYWORD2 =#XF63Ø
            COUNTWORD  =#XCØEØ
            GLOBWORD   =#XAAAA
            LIBRWORD   =#XBBBB
            SECTWORD   =#XE7FF
$)

LET ABORT(CODE, ADDR, OLDSTACK) BE
$(1 WRITEF("*N*NFAULT %N*N", CODE)

    WRITEF("ADDR = #%X4, STACK POINTER = #%X4*N",
           ADDR, OLDSTACK)

    BACKTRACE(ADDR, OLDSTACK)
    MAPSTORE()
    STOP(1ØØ)
$)1

LET BACKTRACE(ADDR, STACKP) BE
$(1 LET P = STACKP
    LET Q, L, F = P+9, Ø, Ø

    WRITES("*NBACKTRACE CALLED*N")

    WRITES("*N      P       LINK      FUNCT?*
           *        VARI      VAR2      . . .*N*N")

    FOR I = 1 TO 25 DO
    $( WRITEF("#%X4: ", P)
       UNLESS 5ØØ<=P<=32ØØØ BREAK
```

```
        L := P!Ø
        WRITEARG(L) // link
        F := P!1-8  // function name?
        TEST (F!-1=LIBRWORD | F!4=ENTRYWORD1) &
             GETBYTE(F,Ø)=7
             THEN WRITEF(" '%S'", F)
             ELSE WRITEF("           ")


        IF Q>P+7 | Q<P DO Q := P+7

        FOR T = P+2 TO Q-1 DO WRITEARG(!T)

        IF P!Ø=Ø & P!1=Ø DO $( WRITES("*NBASE OF STACK*N")
                               BREAK  $)

        UNLESS 5ØØ<=L<=32ØØØ DO
                    $( WRITES("*NIMPROPER LINK*N")
                       BREAK  $)

        NEWLINE()

        Q := P
        P := P - !L    $)
    WRITES("*NEND OF BACKTRACE*N*N")  $)1


LET MAPSTORE() BE
$(1 LET K = Ø  // used for layout

    LET G = GLOBBASE
    LET GSIZE = G!Ø

    WRITEF("STACKBASE=#%X4, STACKEND=#%X4*N",
           STACKBASE, STACKEND)

    WRITEF("*NVALUES SET IN THE GLOBAL VECTOR(#%X4)  ", G)


    TEST 1ØØ<=GSIZE<=1ØØØØ
        THEN WRITEF("%N GLOBALS ALLOCATED*N", GSIZE)
        ELSE $( GSIZE := 4ØØ
                WRITES("GLOBAL ZERO CORRUPTED*N")  $)
```

```
FOR T = 1 TO GSIZE DO
    UNLESS G!T=GLOBWORD DO
        $( IF K REM 4 = Ø DO NEWLINE()
           K := K + 1
           WRITEF(" G%I3 ", T)
           WRITEARG(G!T)  $)

WRITES("*N*N*N")

K := Ø

WRITEF("MAP AND COUNTS FROM #%X4 TO #%X4*N",
        LOADPOINT, ENDPOINT)

FOR P = LOADPOINT TO ENDPOINT-2 DO
$( IF !P=COUNTWORD & (P!1=P+3 | P!1=P-9) DO
   $( IF K REM 4 = Ø DO NEWLINE()
      K := K + 1
      WRITEF("#%X4:%I7    ", P, P!1!Ø)  $)

   IF !P=SECTWORD & GETBYTE(P+2,Ø)=15 DO
   $( WRITEF("*N*N#%X4 SECTION %S  SIZE %N*N",
                        P,          P+2,       P!1-P)
      K := Ø  $)

   IF (P!4=ENTRYWORD1 & P!5=ENTRYWORD2)  |
      P!(-1)=LIBRWORD DO
      IF GETBYTE(P,Ø)=7 DO
      $( IF K REM 4 = Ø DO NEWLINE( )
         K := K + 1
         WRITEF("#%X4/%S  ",   P+4, P)  $)
$)
WRITES("*N*NEND OF MAP*N*N")

$)1


AND WRITEARG(V) BE
$(1 LET F = V  - 4
    IF F!-1=LIBRWORD | V!Ø=ENTRYWORD1 DO
        IF GETBYTE(F,Ø)=7 DO
            $( WRITEF(" '%S'", F)
               RETURN  $)

    WRITEF("     #%X4", V)  $)1
```

5.5 TRACE *and the profile option*

TRACEFN is a procedure which outputs a summary of each activation of the procedures in a program. The summary takes the form of the procedure name, the values of the parameters on entry and the value of the stack pointer on entry. This information is output when the procedure is entered if the global variable TRACING is set to true. An appropriate compiler option (see your implementation notes) will cause calls to TRACEFN to be inserted automatically. Thus you can select the use of TRACEFN by manipulating TRACING, and by using the compiler option, so that only the required tracing output is generated.

The profile option causes additional statistics to be gathered, whilst the program is running, for subsequent output by MAPSTORE. Use of the option causes extra instructions to be compiled to maintain execution counts at certain places in the compiled code. The locations and values of these counts can be related to the original source program with little difficulty. In effect, an execution count for each linear sequence of commands (i.e. the body of a loop, alternatives in conditional commands etc.) is maintained.

The advantages of the profile option include:

1. after a catastrophic error, it indicates those parts of the program that were never executed;
2. it helps to find inner loops and frequently executed sequences;
3. studying the profile counts of a large program tends to increase understanding of the way the program works in practice (e.g. the effectiveness of a freestore-management strategy, or a hashing function);
4. the option is relatively cheap, typically adding 20% to the size and execution time of a program.

5.6 DEBUG: *an interactive debugging system*

DEBUG was written as an interactive debugging aid for BCPL programs running on the ModComp II computer under the MAXCOM system. DEBUG allows one to inspect the state of the BCPL program and read or update any location in store. The user can insert and remove breakpoints in his compiled program, and cause continuation after inspecting variables etc.

DEBUG maintains 17 words of memory consisting of 16 variables V0 to V15 and a special word called the *current value*. The current value can be set by typing a basic expression. Examples of every kind of basic expression are given below:

1265	a decimal number
#7FFD	a hexadecimal number
V3	the value of a variable
V	the address of the vector of variables
G31	the value of a global variable
G	the base of the global vector

The current value can be modified by typing an operator and possibly a second basic expression. Operators available are: +, −, *, /, ? (remainder after division), < (left shift), > (right shift), &, % (logical-or), ! (indirection; . is a synonym for !). Complicated expressions may be typed, but parentheses are not permitted and evaluation is strictly left to right.

Commands are identified by a single character. Typical commands (in all some 18 are available) are:

=	print the value of the current expression in the currently selected style;
C, H, O, D	used to select the printing style for values;
:	print the contents of the location addressed by the current value;
U	update a general store location;
Sn	update variable Vn;
Pn	update global n;
L	list a region of store;
X	call a specified BCPL procedure with up to five arguments;
Fn	search store for a specified value;
Bn	set or unset breakpoint n;
Q	exit from DEBUG (continue after breakpoint).

Even though DEBUG is machine dependent, it is a good example of a small yet powerful facility, and the following code can form a useful basis for similar systems on many other machines.

```
GET "LIBHDR"

GLOBAL $( GLOBØ:Ø  $)

MANIFEST $(
INSTR.SIR.3=#X2683
$)

STATIC $( CH=Ø; VARS=Ø; STYLE=Ø; GLOBBASE=Ø
          INSTR=Ø; ADDR=Ø
          REC.P=Ø; REC.L=Ø  $)

LET DEBUG() = VALOF
$(1 LET A = Ø
    LET RDCHSAV, WRCHSAV = RDCH, WRCH

    VARS  := TABLE Ø,Ø,Ø,Ø,Ø,Ø,Ø,Ø,Ø,Ø,Ø,Ø,Ø,Ø,Ø,Ø
    INSTR := TABLE Ø,Ø,Ø,Ø,Ø,Ø,Ø,Ø,Ø,Ø
    ADDR  := TABLE Ø,Ø,Ø,Ø,Ø,Ø,Ø,Ø,Ø,Ø
    STYLE := "  %X4"
    GLOBBASE := @GLOBØ
    REC.P, REC.L := LEVEL(), NXT
```

```
        TEST STANDALONE
        THEN $( LET BREAKNO = -1
                FOR I = Ø TO 9 DO
                        IF !#X26=ADDR!I+1 DO BREAKNO := I
                RDCH, WRCH := SORDCH, SOWRCH
                TEST BREAKNO<Ø
                THEN WRITES("*NSTANDALONE DEBUG*N")
                ELSE $( LET SIZE = INSTRSIZE(INSTR!BREAKNO)
                        LET T = TABLE Ø,Ø,Ø,Ø,Ø,Ø
                        A := ADDR!BREAKNO
                        T!Ø := INSTR!BREAKNO
                        FOR I = 1 TO SIZE-1 DO T!I := A!I
                        T!SIZE := #XE7ØØ  // BRU
                        T!(SIZE+1) := A + SIZE
                        !#X26 := T  // plug resumption address
                        WRITEF("BREAK NO %N AT %X4*N", BREAKNO, A)
                    $)
            $)
        ELSE WRITES("*NDEBUG*N")

NXT:CH := RDCH()

SW: SWITCHON CH INTO
    $( DEFAULT: ERROR("BAD COMMAND %C", CH)

        CASE '*N':
        CASE '*S': GOTO NXT

        CASE '#':CASE 'V':CASE 'G':
        CASE 'Ø':CASE '1':CASE '2':CASE '3':CASE '4':
        CASE '5':CASE '6':CASE '7':CASE '8':CASE '9':
                A := RBEXP()
                GOTO SW

        CASE '.':CASE '!':CASE '+':CASE '-':CASE '**':
        CASE '/':CASE '?':CASE '<':CASE '>':
        CASE '&':CASE '%':
                A := REXP(A)
                GOTO SW
        CASE 'C': STYLE := " %C";  GOTO NXT
        CASE 'H': STYLE := " %X4"; GOTO NXT
        CASE 'O': STYLE := " %O6"; GOTO NXT
        CASE 'D': STYLE := " %I6"; GOTO NXT
```

```
CASE 'X': A := A(VARS!Ø,VARS!1,VARS!2,VARS!3,VARS!4)
          GOTO NXT

CASE 'U': CH := RDCH()
          !A := REXP(RBEXP())
          GOTO SW

CASE 'I': A := A+1
          GOTO NXT

CASE 'L': CH := RDCH()
          FOR I = Ø TO RBEXP()-1 DO
          $( IF I REM 8 = Ø DO $( NEWLINE()
                                        PRADDR(A+I)  $)
             WRITEF(STYLE,A!I)  $)
          NEWLINE()
          GOTO NXT

CASE '=': WRITEF(STYLE, A)
          NEWLINE()
          GOTO NXT

CASE 'N': A := A+1
CASE ':': WRITEF(STYLE, !A)
          NEWLINE()
          GOTO NXT

CASE 'B': // Ø B      unset all break points
          // Ø Bn     unset break point n
          // A Bn     set break point n to addr A
$( LET N = -1
   CH := RDCH()
   IF 'Ø'<=CH<='9' DO
   $( N := CH-'Ø'
      CH := RDCH()    $)

   IF A=Ø DO
   $( FOR I = Ø TO 9 DO IF I=N | N<Ø DO
           IF ADDR!I NE Ø DO
           $( !(ADDR!I) := INSTR!I  // UNSET BREAK PT
              ADDR!I := Ø  $)
      GOTO SW  $)

   IF INSTRSIZE(!A)=Ø | N<Ø | ADDR!N NE Ø DO
                    ERROR("BAD BREAK")
```

```
              INSTR!N, ADDR!N := !A, A
              !A := INSTR.SIR.3
              GOTO SW
          $)

      CASE 'F': $( LET W, M = VARS!Ø, VARS!1
                  CH := RDCH()
                  FOR I = 1 TO RBEXP() DO
                  $( IF ((!A NEQV W)&M)=Ø GOTO SW
                      A := A+1  $)
                  WRITES("BAD FIND")
                  GOTO SW  $)

      CASE 'P': CH := RDCH()
                GLOBBASE!RDN(1Ø) := A
                GOTO SW

      CASE 'S': CH := RDCH()
                VARS!RDVN() := A
                GOTO SW

      CASE 'T': BACKTRACE(Ø, A); GOTO NXT

      CASE 'M': NEWLINE()
                MAPSTORE()
                GOTO NXT

      CASE 'Q': WRITES(" EXIT FROM DEBUG*N")
                RDCH, WRCH := RDCHSAV, WRCHSAV
                RESULTIS A
      $)
$)1

AND RDN(RADIX) = VALOF
$(1 LET A, SW = Ø, FALSE

    $( LET D = -1
       IF 'Ø'<=CH<='9' DO D := CH-'Ø'
       IF 'A'<=CH<='F' DO D := 1Ø+CH-'A'
       UNLESS Ø<=D<RADIX BREAK
       SW := TRUE
       A := A*RADIX + D
       CH := RDCH()  $) REPEAT
```

```
         UNLESS SW DO ERROR("BAD NUMBER")
         RESULTIS A  $)1

AND RDVN() = VALOF
$(1 LET A = RDN(1Ø)
         UNLESS Ø<=A<=15 DO ERROR("BAD VARIABLE")
         RESULTIS A  $)1

AND RBEXP() = VALOF SWITCHON CH INTO
$(1 DEFAULT:  ERROR("BAD EXPRESSION")

    CASE 'Ø':CASE '1':CASE '2':CASE '3':CASE '4':
    CASE '5':CASE '6':CASE '7':CASE '8':CASE '9':
                RESULTIS RDN(1Ø)

    CASE '#': CH := RDCH()
                RESULTIS RDN(16)

    CASE 'G': CH := RDCH()
                UNLESS 'Ø'<=CH<='9' RESULTIS GLOBBASE
                RESULTIS GLOBBASE!RDN(1Ø)

    CASE 'V': CH := RDCH()
                UNLESS 'Ø'<=CH<='9' RESULTIS VARS
                RESULTIS VARS!RDVN()

    CASE '-': CH := RDCH(); RESULTIS -RBEXP()
    CASE '+': CH := RDCH(); RESULTIS  RBEXP()
$)1

AND B() = VALOF $( CH := RDCH()
                    RESULTIS RBEXP()  $)


AND REXP(A) = VALOF
$(1 SWITCHON CH INTO

    $( DEFAULT:   RESULTIS A

       CASE '.':
       CASE '!':  A := !A; CH := RDCH(); LOOP
       CASE '+':  A := A+B();     LOOP
       CASE '-':  A := A-B();     LOOP
       CASE '**': A := A*B();     LOOP
       CASE '/':  A := A/B();     LOOP
       CASE '?':  A := A REM B(); LOOP
```

```
        CASE '<': A := A<<B( );      LOOP
        CASE '>': A := A>>B( );      LOOP
        CASE '&': A := A&B( );       LOOP
        CASE '%': A := A|B( );       LOOP
    $)
$)1 REPEAT

AND PRADDR(A) BE
$(1 A := A & #77777
    TEST GLOBBASE<=A<=GLOBBASE+GLOBBASE!Ø
    THEN WRITEF(" G%I3 ", A-GLOBBASE)
    ELSE TEST VARS<=A<=VARS+15
         THEN WRITEF(" V%12# ", A-VARS)
         ELSE WRITEF("%I6", A)
    WRITEF("(%X4): ", A)  $)1

AND INSTRSIZE(INS) = VALOF
$(1 LET F = INS>>8
    LET T = TABLE // 2 bits per op code
                  // O if unbreakable otherwise the size
                  // except for CBMB and CRMB
            #X554Ø,#X5555,       Ø,      Ø,
            #X5555,#X5555,#X5555,#XAAAA,
            #X5555,#X5551,       Ø,      Ø,
            #X5555,#X5551,#XAAAA,#XAAAA,
            #XA8FC,      Ø,#X54AB,#X54AB,
            #XAØAØ,#XØØØF,#X5Ø5Ø,#X5Ø5Ø,
            #XA8FC,      Ø,#X54AB,#X54AB,
            #XAAAA,#XAAA8,#X5554,#X5555

    IF F=#X87 | F=#XC7 RESULTIS 4    // CBMB or CRMB

    IF F=#XE7 & (INS&#XFØ) NE Ø RESULTIS Ø
                                 // BLM is unbreakable

    RESULTIS T!(F>>3)>>14-2*(F&7) & 3
$)1

AND ERROR(S, A) BE
$(1 NEWLINE( )
    WRITEF(S, A)
    NEWLINE( )
    UNTIL CH='*N' DO CH := RDCH( )
    LONGJUMP(REC.P, REC.L)  $)1
```

5.7   Runtime potholes and traps

Even the most careful programmer will occasionally be baffled by some runtime errors, and the inexperienced newcomer will undoubtedly experience greatest difficulty here. However, he should take encouragement from the fact that BCPL is an order of magnitude easier to write and debug than assembly code, and that many large BCPL programs have been made to run with little difficulty.

We now discuss some of the more common causes of perplexity that have been noted by those engaged in introducing and teaching BCPL.

5.7.1   Missing procedure

This is a frequent cause of problems and can occur, for example, if a global procedure is omitted altogether, or its name is mistyped in its declaration. The declaration of a global variable at the head of a program allows the compiler to accept calls to a procedure with this name from any part of the program. The compiler assumes that the global variable will contain, at the time of call, the procedure value (normally the entry address) of the procedure. There is no check that the procedure has in fact been provided, indeed it may well be presented as part of a separately compiled module. Omission of the procedure altogether will usually cause the program to abort in some implementation-dependent way, often generating a post-mortem dump.

5.7.2   Erroneous allocation of global variables

It is neither possible nor desirable for the compiler to check that global variables have been allocated distinct locations in the global vector. Hence it is possible for the same global location to be used accidentally for two purposes at the same time, possibly as the result of mistyping a global number. A possible effect of this error is that either the wrong procedure is called, or the procedure value is destroyed, or the value of a variable is unexpectedly changed.

5.7.3   Misuse of procedure values

In some languages (e.g. Algol 60), you assign to the function name as a method of specifying the result of the function call. This is not the case in BCPL, since the body of a function is an expression (usually a valof-expression). However, it is not uncommon for newcomers to BCPL to assign to the function name. This results in the destruction of the procedure value (i.e. the function's start address), almost certainly causing a catastrophic fault the next time the function is called. Omitting the brackets in a parameterless function call will produce the procedure value of the function, not the result of calling it.

5.7.4 Misuse of pointers and subscripts

This error is frequently committed. The result is often spectacular, as vectors are usually stored on a stack together with procedure links and dynamic variables. Corruption of a link can cause unexpected jumps and loops. Sometimes this error simply results in the values of other variables being mysteriously altered. If a procedure value is corrupted to zero then on some implementations this can result in re-entry to the entire program. Corruption of the stack can also devalue the effectiveness of runtime tracing and post-mortem systems. On some implementations it is possible to overwrite the program if a subscript is out of bounds by a substantial amount, or if a vector or pointer is used before it is initialised.

5.7.5 Simultaneous declarations

The facility in BCPL to declare several variables and procedures simultaneously can lead to unexpected results, illustrated by the following example:

```
LET A = 5
AND B = A + 2
```

This is, in fact, unlikely to place the value 7 in B. The assignments implied in the declaration may be performed in either order. This can lead to a program working on one installation but not another. The AND construction is never needed for simple variables and should only be used when really necessary for procedures.

5.7.6 Multiple use of the same name

It is easy to forget that a local variable will take precedence over a global of the same name. Note also that (unlike many other programming languages) the following block contains two separate variables I:

```
$( LET I = Ø
   . . .
   FOR I = Ø  TO 5 DO
   $( . . .  //   only the controlled variable I
             //   of the for-command is accessible here
   $)
   . . .     //   and the original I will have the same
             //   value as it had before the for-loop
$)
```

5.7.7   Effects of BCPL call-by-value

An easy trap for ex-Fortran programmers is to assign to a formal parameter inside a procedure, expecting this to result in an assignment to the actual parameter. It does not.

5.7.8   Erroneous use of GOTO

Ex-Algol programmers tend to forget that a BCPL goto-command cannot be used to cause the logical termination of a procedure (unwinding the stack etc.). If this is attempted the program often continues to run for some time without obvious error until it collapses mysteriously. In normal BCPL programs, the experienced programmer finds that he does not need to use GOTO very often, and when he does it is almost always to a label within the same procedure. In the rare cases when exit from a procedure using the effect of GOTO is perceived as necessary, then the library procedures LEVEL and LONGJUMP should be used (see chapter four).

5.7.9   ENDCASE

If ENDCASE is omitted at the end of a group of commands labelled by a case-label within a switchon-command, then control passes through to the next CASE. Curious effects can result from accidental omission of ENDCASE.

5.7.10   The dangling-reference problem

This problem occurs when the address of some dynamic variable (or perhaps a vector) in a procedure is preserved, say, in a global. Subsequently an exit is made from the procedure, and then the global is used. The result is a reference to a variable which the compiler has deallocated.

5.7.11   Omission of operators

Some newcombers to BCPL find it difficult to remember that vectors in BCPL are accessed as V!(N+1), not as V(N+1) or V[N+1]. The compiler treats both of the latter as a call on the function V. Equally, writing

```
A + 4 (B + C)
```

instead of

```
A + 4 * (B + C)
```

will cause, on many implementations, a subroutine jump to location 4 of the machine.

5.7.12   Operator precedence errors

In a typeless language we have to consider the relative precedence of operators that normally have no relation with each other. For example, consider

```
A+1 << N   and   A + 1<<N
```

Intuitively they mean different things. Syntactically they are equivalent, and in fact both mean (A+1)<<N as + takes precedence over <<. A similar source of errors is in expressions such as contained in

```
IF A&#77 = B&#77 DO  . . .
```

This means

```
IF (A & (#77=B)) & #77 DO  . . .
```

If A happens to match the representation for false, or if A matches true and B is not equal to #77, then the condition will be false. Otherwise the result is implementation dependent! The precedence rules of BCPL cannot be blamed, as the following example shows:

```
IF A='X' & B='Y' DO  . . .
```

This time the intuitive meaning is correct:

```
IF (A='X') & (B='Y') DO  . . .
```

5.7.13   Parameter mismatches

It is easy to forget, after using Algol or PL/I, that there is no type-checking of BCPL parameters, or indeed that the desired number of parameters has been provided.

5.7.14   *Uninitialised variables*

The initial contents of vectors and globals are not defined in BCPL. In many
implementations, the store locations corresponding to the global vector might be
initialised to zero or some other value (e.g. the address of ABORT, to trap the
missing procedure error described above). Vectors use re-usable store so this
certainly should not be relied upon. In general the store will contain rubbish
which will vary from run to run. If your program behaves differently every time
you run it, or only sometimes works, then this could well be a sign that a location is
being used before being initialised.

5.7.15   *Selecting the wrong output*

Great care should be taken to ensure that the correct output stream is selected at
all times. This is particularly the case when diagnostics are being generated. It is
easy to mix diagnostics with other output. If this output is binary, then the
program simply generates corrupt binary output with no visible indication why.

6

The BCPL lexical and syntax analyser

In this chapter a substantial body of BCPL text is presented and discussed in detail. It consists of an important part of the BCPL compiler and has been included here for many reasons. In the first place, it is a realistic example of how BCPL is used in practice. It has been carefully written and is used to exhibit various points relating to programming style in BCPL and it also contains many examples of programming techniques that are well suited to BCPL. In addition, the complete understanding of this program helps to consolidate one's knowledge of the BCPL syntax. It is also likely to be useful to those people involved in writing compilers in high-level languages, particularly if they plan to use BCPL for the purpose.

Before describing the syntax analyser in detail, it is necessary to give a brief description of the overall structure of the compiler in order to clarify the context in which the syntax analyser runs. The compiler is implemented in three passes called SYN, TRN and CG as shown in figure 6.1.

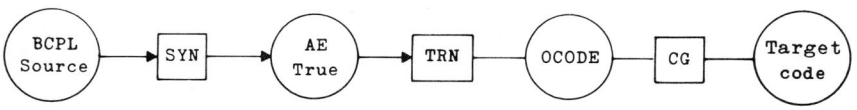

Fig. 6.1   The structure of the BCPL compiler

SYN is the pass that performs the syntax analysis of the raw BCPL source and converts it into the tree structure held in main memory called the *applicative expression tree* (AE tree). This tree is then processed by the translation phase TRN to produce a linear sequence of statements in an intermediate code called OCODE. The OCODE form is then translated into either relocatable binary or assembly code for the target machine by the code generator (CG). OCODE has been carefully designed so that it can be translated with reasonable efficiency into the machine codes of most computers. It is described in detail in the next chapter. All three passes are normally coded in BCPL. Although the code generator must necessarily be different for different computers, the passes SYN and TRN are almost entirely machine independent and so this part of the compiler is nearly the same for each implementation of BCPL.

6.1   The lexical analyser

When compiling BCPL it is convenient to break up the raw source text of the program into a sequence of the basic symbols of the language. There are about 75 such symbols, many of which are represented by reserved words, such as LET and RETURN. Numerical constants, string constants, and identifiers are regarded as basic symbols, and so are composite symbols such as := and ->. The lexical analyser is implemented as a routine NEXTSYMB which is called by the syntax analyser whenever it requires another basic symbol from the source program. The syntax analyser does no backtracking. That is, it performs the analysis while reading the basic symbols in one at a time without having to reconsider a symbol previously dealt with.

Within the compiler, the basic symbols are represented by small positive integers as specified in the manifest declaration appearing in the syntax-analyser header file given in lines 1 to 60 of the listing. Thus, for instance, S.GE (=25), declared on line 10, is used to denote the basic symbol >=. The use of manifest constants for this purpose is extremely beneficial to the readability of the program by eliminating the need for the programmer to remember which integer corresponds to which basic symbol. Such manifest constants are often used in case-labels to good effect.

```
 1 //    SYNHDR
 2
 3 GET "LIBHDR"
 4
 5 MANIFEST $(   // AE tree operators
 6 S.NUMBER=1; S.NAME=2; S.STRING=3; S.TRUE=4; S.FALSE=5
 7 S.VALOF=6; S.LV=7; S.RV=8; S.VECAP=9; S.FNAP=1Ø
 8 S.MULT=11; S.DIV=12; S.REM=13
 9 S.PLUS=14; S.MINUS=15; S.NEG=17
1Ø S.EQ=2Ø; S.NE=21; S.LS=22; S.GR=23; S.LE=24; S.GE=25
11 S.NOT=3Ø; S.LSHIFT=31; S.RSHIFT=32; S.LOGAND=33; S.LOGOR=34
12 S.EQV=35; S.NEQV=36; S.COND=37; S.COMMA=38; S.TABLE=39
13 S.AND=4Ø; S.VALDEF=41; S.VECDEF=42; S.CONSTDEF=43
14 S.FNDEF=44; S.RTDEF=45
15 S.ASS=5Ø; S.RTAP=51; S.GOTO=52; S.RESULTIS=53; S.COLON=54
16 S.TEST=55; S.FOR=56; S.IF=57; S.UNLESS=58
17 S.WHILE=59; S.UNTIL=6Ø; S.REPEAT=61; S.REPEATWHILE=62
18 S.REPEATUNTIL=63
19 S.LOOP=65; S.BREAK=66; S.RETURN=67; S.FINISH=68
2Ø S.ENDCASE=69; S.SWITCHON=7Ø; S.CASE=71; S.DEFAULT=72
21 S.SEQ=73; S.LET=74; S.MANIFEST=75; S.GLOBAL=76; S.STATIC=79
22
23 // other basic symbol codes
24 S.BE=89; S.END=9Ø; S.LSECT=91; S.RSECT=92; S.GET=93
25 S.SEMICOLON=97; S.INTO=98
26 S.TO=99; S.BY=1ØØ; S.DO=1Ø1; S.OR=1Ø2
27 S.VEC=1Ø3; S.LPAREN=1Ø5; S.RPAREN=1Ø6
28 $)
29
3Ø GLOBAL $(    // globals used in LEX
31 CHBUF:1ØØ; DECVAL:1Ø1
32 GETV:1Ø3; GETP:1Ø4; GETT:1Ø5
33 WORDV:1Ø6; WORDSIZE:1Ø7; CHARV:1Ø8; CHARP:1Ø9
34 PRSOURCE:11Ø; PRLINE:111; READNUMBER:112; RDSTRCH:113
35 SYMB:115; WORDNODE:116; CH:117
36 RDTAG:118; PERFORMGET:119
37 NEXTSYMB:12Ø; DECLSYSWORDS:121; NLPENDING:122; CODEP:123
38 LOOKUPWORD:125; RCH:126; LEXTRACE:127; OPTION:128
39 WRCHBUF:131; CHCOUNT:132; LINECOUNT:133
4Ø NULLTAG:134; REC.P:135; REC.L:136
41
```

NEXTSYMB is a parameterless routine which causes the global variable SYMB to be set to the integer code for the next basic symbol of the source program each time it is called. On entry the global variable CH contains the next character of the source stream and on exit it holds the first character following the Basic symbol recognised.

For some symbols, additional information is passed in the variables DECVAL, WORDSIZE and WORDNODE. If the basic symbol was the first symbol to appear on a line, then the global variable NLPENDING contains the value true. The definition of NEXTSYMB is given starting at line 65 of the listing.

After initialising NLPENDING to false, NEXTSYMB switches on the character in CH and takes appropriate action as described below.

The characters tab, newline and space are ignorable and are read in until the first non-ignorable character is found. While reading newpage and newline, it is necessary to increment the line count and set the NLPENDING flag to true. This flag is used in the syntax-analyser routine REXP to deal with the rule concerning a dyadic operator occurring as the first symbol of a line (see page 114). If the character is a digit, then it starts a decimal number. The number is read in and evaluated using the routine READNUMBER which is described later. On exit from READNUMBER, CH will already contain the next character of the source program and so NEXTSYMB returns directly.

```
42 // globals used in SYN
43 RDBLOCKBODY:14Ø; RDSECT:141
44 RNAMELIST:142; RNAME:143
45 REXP:144; RDEF:145; RCOM:146
46 RDCDEFS:147; NAMETABLE:148
47 FORMTREE:15Ø; SYNREPORT:151; PLIST:152
48 CHECKFOR:153; IGNORE:154; REXPLIST:155; RDSEQ:156
49 LIST1:161; LIST2:162; LIST3:163
5Ø LIST4:164; LIST5:165; LIST6:166
51 NEWVEC:167; TREEP:168; TREEVEC:169
52 CHARCODE:19Ø; REPORTCOUNT:191; REPORTMAX:192
53 SOURCESTREAM:193
54 $)
55
56 MANIFEST $(     //  selectors
57 H1=Ø; H2=1; H3=2; H4=3; H5=4; H6=5
58 NAMETABLESIZE=1ØØ
59 $)
6Ø .
61 //     LEX1
62
63 GET "SYNHDR"
64
65 LET NEXTSYMB() BE
66 $(1 NLPENDING := FALSE
67
68 $(2 IF LEXTRACE DO WRCH(CH)
69
7Ø      SWITCHON CH INTO
71
72 $(S CASE '*P':
73     CASE '*N': LINECOUNT := LINECOUNT + 1
74            NLPENDING := TRUE // ignorable characters
75     CASE '*T':
76     CASE '*S': RCH() REPEATWHILE CH='*S'
77                LOOP
78
79     CASE 'Ø':CASE '1':CASE '2':CASE '3':CASE '4':
8Ø     CASE '5':CASE '6':CASE '7':CASE '8':CASE '9':
81         SYMB := S.NUMBER
82         READNUMBER(1Ø)
83         RETURN
84
```

If CH is in the range A to Z, then it starts either a name or a system word; in either case, the characters of the word are read and packed into the vector WORDV by a call of RDTAG. The word is then looked up in a symbol table using the function LOOKUPWORD. This function deals with both reserved words and identifiers and is described later. If the symbol happens to be the reserved word GET, then the get-directive is obeyed by a call of PERFORMGET. Both opening and closing section brackets begin with the character $ and can have a tag composed of the same characters that may appear in identifiers. It is therefore natural to use the routine RDTAG to read in this tag. The argument to RDTAG is normally the first character of an identifier, but, when it is used to read a section-bracket tag, the character $ is passed as an artificial first character to eliminate any possible confusion with other identifiers or system words when the tag is looked up in the symbol table by LOOKUPWORD.

Many characters (e.g. + ; & = !) correspond directly to basic symbols and are handled simply. For example, the code for + is on line 117. Before returning from NEXTSYMB, it is necessary to update CH with the next character of input, and this is achieved by executing the call of RCH which occurs at the end of the body of NEXTSYMB. This point is reached by executing the command BREAK.

```
85      CASE 'A':CASE 'B':CASE 'C':CASE 'D':CASE 'E':
86      CASE 'F':CASE 'G':CASE 'H':CASE 'I':CASE 'J':
87      CASE 'K':CASE 'L':CASE 'M':CASE 'N':CASE 'O':
88      CASE 'P':CASE 'Q':CASE 'R':CASE 'S':CASE 'T':
89      CASE 'U':CASE 'V':CASE 'W':CASE 'X':CASE 'Y':
90      CASE 'Z':
91          RDTAG(CH)
92          SYMB := LOOKUPWORD()
93          IF SYMB=S.GET DO $( PERFORMGET(); LOOP  $)
94          RETURN
95
96      CASE '$': RCH()
97              UNLESS CH='(' | CH=')' DO SYNREPORT(91)
98              SYMB := CH='(' -> S.LSECT, S.RSECT
99              RDTAG('$')
100             LOOKUPWORD()
101             RETURN
102
103     CASE '[':
104     CASE '(': SYMB := S.LPAREN; BREAK
105     CASE ']':
106     CASE ')': SYMB := S.RPAREN; BREAK
107
108     CASE '#':
109         SYMB := S.NUMBER
110         RCH()
111         IF '0'<=CH<='7' DO  $( READNUMBER(8);  RETURN  $)
112         IF CH='B' DO $( RCH(); READNUMBER(2);  RETURN  $)
113         IF CH='O' DO $( RCH(); READNUMBER(8);  RETURN  $)
114         IF CH='X' DO $( RCH(); READNUMBER(16); RETURN  $)
115         SYNREPORT(33)
116
117     CASE '+': SYMB := S.PLUS;      BREAK
118     CASE ',': SYMB := S.COMMA;     BREAK
119     CASE ';': SYMB := S.SEMICOLON; BREAK
120     CASE '@': SYMB := S.LV;        BREAK
121     CASE '&': SYMB := S.LOGAND;    BREAK
122     CASE '|': SYMB := S.LOGOR;     BREAK
123     CASE '=': SYMB := S.EQ;        BREAK
124     CASE '!': SYMB := S.VECAP;     BREAK
125     CASE '**':SYMB := S.MULT;      BREAK
126
```

Certain other characters (e.g. – < :) can start composite basic symbols and the treatment of these is exemplified by the program for < on line 154.

```
127      CASE '/':
128          RCH()
129          IF CH='\' DO $( SYMB := S.LOGAND; BREAK $)
130          IF CH='/' DO
131              $( RCH() REPEATUNTIL CH='*N' | CH=ENDSTREAMCH
132                  LOOP  $)
133
134          UNLESS CH='**' DO $( SYMB := S.DIV; RETURN  $)
135
136          $( RCH()
137              IF CH='**' DO
138                  $( RCH() REPEATWHILE CH='**'
139                      IF CH='/' BREAK  $)
140              IF CH='*N' DO LINECOUNT := LINECOUNT+1
141              IF CH=ENDSTREAMCH DO SYNREPORT(63)
142          $) REPEAT
143
144          RCH()
145          LOOP
146
147
148      CASE '\': RCH()
149              IF CH='/' DO $( SYMB := S.LOGOR;  BREAK $)
150              IF CH='=' DO $( SYMB := S.NE;     BREAK $)
151              SYMB := S.NOT
152              RETURN
153
154      CASE '<': RCH()
155              IF CH='=' DO $( SYMB := S.LE;     BREAK $)
156              IF CH='<' DO $( SYMB := S.LSHIFT; BREAK $)
157              SYMB := S.LS
158              RETURN
159
160      CASE '>': RCH()
161              IF CH='=' DO $( SYMB := S.GE;     BREAK $)
162              IF CH='>' DO $( SYMB := S.RSHIFT; BREAK $)
163              SYMB := S.GR
164              RETURN
165
166      CASE '-': RCH()
167              IF CH='>' DO $( SYMB := S.COND; BREAK  $)
168              SYMB := S.MINUS
169              RETURN
170
```

String constants are enclosed in double quotes and may contain up to 255 string characters. These characters are read using the function RDSTRCH and are stored in the vector CHARV one by one. These characters are then packed into the vector WORDV using the library procedure PACKSTRING. The result of this call is assigned to WORDSIZE, being the subscript of the highest element of WORDV that is used in the packed string. One should note that this part of the lexical analyser will work whatever the word length of the machine on which the compiler is running, since the machine-dependent knowledge of how strings are packed is entirely encapsulated in the library routine PACKSTRING. PACKSTRING is used for the same purpose in RDTAG in the treatment of identifiers and section bracket tags.

A character constant is a string character enclosed in single quotes and is semantically equivalent to a number. The value of the number must be known early in the compilation since character constants can be used in manifest expressions. But since it depends on the character code of the target machine, which may be different from the code used in the compiling machine, it is necessary to perform a code conversion. This is done by the function CHARCODE which is set up in the steering program of the compiler. CHARCODE is also used in TRN to convert the codes of string characters as they are converted into OCODE form.

Either a dot or an end-of-stream character can mark the end of a section of program. If the current input is from a get-stream (see page 96), then the previous input is resumed, otherwise the end of the program is indicated by setting SYMB to the value S.END. Notice that illegal characters cause a syntax error message to be generated, by the call SYNREPORT(94) and that this call is made after assigning the character '*S' to CH in order to prevent an infinite repetition of this error message.

```
171     CASE ':': RCH()
172               IF CH='=' DO $( SYMB := S.ASS; BREAK  $)
173               SYMB := S.COLON
174               RETURN
175
176
177     CASE '"': CHARP := Ø
178               RCH()
179
180               UNTIL CH='"' DO
181                   $( IF CHARP=255 DO SYNREPORT(34)
182                      CHARP := CHARP + 1
183                      CHARV!CHARP := RDSTRCH()  $)
184
185               CHARV!Ø := CHARP
186               WORDSIZE := PACKSTRING(CHARV, WORDV)
187               SYMB := S.STRING
188               BREAK
189
190     CASE '*'':RCH()
191               DECVAL := CHARCODE(RDSTRCH())
192               SYMB := S.NUMBER
193               UNLESS CH='*'' DO SYNREPORT(34)
194               BREAK
195
196
197     DEFAULT:  UNLESS CH=ENDSTREAMCH DO $( CH := '*S'
198                                          SYNREPORT(94) $)
199     CASE '.': IF GETP=Ø DO $( SYMB := S.END
200                               RETURN   $)
201               ENDREAD()
202               GETP := GETP - 3
203               SOURCESTREAM := GETV!GETP
204               SELECTINPUT(SOURCESTREAM)
205               LINECOUNT := GETV!(GETP+1)
206               CH := GETV!(GETP+2)
207               LOOP
208 $)S
209
210 $)2 REPEAT
211
212     RCH()
213 $)1
```

6.2   The function LOOKUPWORD

Identifiers, system words, and section bracket tags are held in a symbol table maintained by the lexical analyser. This table is organised as a number of lists whose roots are the elements of a vector called NAMETABLE. When a name is to be looked up in this table, the function LOOKUPWORD is called with the packed characters of the name held in the elements of WORDV. The subscript of the highest element of WORDV that is used is held in the variable WORDSIZE. In order to select which list to search, LOOKUPWORD computes a simple hash value (on line 223) that depends on the characters in WORDV. It does this by adding together the first and last words of WORDV as though they were integers, shifting to the right by one place and then using REM to obtain the result after division by the name table size. This hash-value computation has been designed with care in order to ensure that it works reasonably well whatever character code, word length or number representation is being used. It should be observed that the hash value depends upon the length and first few characters of the name, since these are held in WORDV!Ø, and also the last few characters of the name, since these are held in WORDV!WORDSIZE. The logical right shift is used to ensure that the left-hand operand of REM is positive thus assuring a positive hash value. NAMETABLESIZE is currently declared as a manifest constant equal to 100. It is clear that the same name may give rise to different hash values on many different implementations of BCPL, but this does not stop the algorithm from working effectively.

The first word of a name node contains the integer code of the basic symbol that this node represents. It is, for instance, the manifest constant S.LET in the node for the system word LET. For an ordinary identifier, it is the manifest constant S.NAME. The second word in a name node is either zero or a pointer to the name node of another name having the same hash value. The third and subsequent words of a name node contain the packed characters of the name. The until-command in LOOKUPWORD controls the search for a node that matches the name held in WORDV. Within this loop, WORDNODE points to the current name node under consideration, and the auxiliary variable I is the subscript of the next element of WORDV to be compared. If the comparision is successful, then I is incremented, otherwise attention is transferred to the next name node in the list. The loop continues either until WORDNODE is zero indicating that the list is exhausted, or until I is greater than WORDSIZE indicating that a matching node has been encountered. In the former case, LOOKUPWORD creates an appropriate new name node and inserts it at the start of the current list. The space for this node is obtained by a call for the function NEWVEC which is described later.

The result of LOOKUPWORD is the integer code for the basic symbol that has just been looked up. Notice that this is extracted from the current name node by the expression H1!WORDNODE in which H1 is a manifest constant equal to zero. The manifest constants H1, H2, . . . , H5 are used as selectors in this way throughout the compiler.

```
214
215 .
216 //    LEX2
217
218 GET "SYNHDR"
219
220 LET LOOKUPWORD() = VALOF
221
222 $(1 LET HASHVAL =
223         (WORDV!Ø+WORDV!WORDSIZE >> 1) REM NAMETABLESIZE
224
225     LET I = Ø
226
227     WORDNODE := NAMETABLE!HASHVAL
228
229     UNTIL WORDNODE=Ø | I>WORDSIZE DO
230            TEST WORDNODE!(I+2)=WORDV!I
231              THEN I := I+1
232              ELSE WORDNODE, I := H2!WORDNODE, Ø
233
234     IF WORDNODE=Ø DO
235     $( WORDNODE := NEWVEC(WORDSIZE+2)
236        WORDNODE!Ø, WORDNODE!1 := S.NAME, NAMETABLE!HASHVAL
237        FOR I = TO WORDSIZE DO WORDNODE!(I+2):= WORDV!I
238        NAMETABLE!HASHVAL := WORDNODE  $)
239
240     RESULTS H1!WORDNODE  $)1
241
242 AND DECLSYSWORDS() BE
243 $(1 CODEP := TABLE
244        S.AND,
245        S.BE,S.BREAK,S.BY,
246        S.CASE,
247        S.DO,S.DEFAULT,
248        S.EQ,S.EQV,S.OR,S.ENDCASE,
249        S.FALSE,S.FOR,S.FINISH,
250        S.GOTO,S.GE,S.GR,S.GLOBAL,S.GET,
251        S.IF,S.INTO,
252        S.LET,S.LV,S.LE,S.LS,
253        S.LOGOR,S.LOGAND,S.LOOP,S.LSHIFT,
```

If we look more closely at the coding of the until-command, we find that it is not entirely optimal since WORDNODE is compared with zero each time I is incremented, and I is compared with WORDSIZE each time I is set to zero. Furthermore, WORDNODE is again compared with zero as soon as the until-loop is terminated although its value is known at that time as a result of the evaluation of the termination condition. The program was written this way since it was the most comprehensible coding that could be found and the slight execution inefficiency is insignificant. To achieve the more efficient coding one would have had to complicate the text by the use of labels and goto-commands.

Before the compilation of a program can be started, it is necessary to initialise the name table with entries for all the reserved words of the language. This is done by a call for the routine DECLSYSWORDS and, since this is called only once, it was worthwhile coding as compactly as possible. The method chosen makes use of a table containing the integer codes for all the reserved-word basic symbols and an auxiliary routine D which unpicks the reserved words, one at a time, from a string of them supplied as its argument. It is necessary to make two calls for D since the string of reserved words would otherwise be too long. The definition of D is straightforward. Note the use of LOOKUPWORD to insert the reserved words into the table.

The last node to be added by DECLSYSWORDS is one representing the (null) tag of an untagged section bracket. The pointer to this last node is assigned to the variable NULLTAG which is used during syntax analysis by the function RDSECT described later.

```
254          S.MANIFEST,
255          S.NE,S.NOT,S.NEQV,
256          S.OR,
257          S.RESULTIS,S.RETURN,S.REM,S.RSHIFT,S.RV,
258          S.REPEAT,S.REPEATWHILE,S.REPEATUNTIL,
259          S.SWITCHON,S.STATIC,
260          S.TO,S.TEST,S.TRUE,S.DO,S.TABLE,
261          S.UNTIL,S.UNLESS,
262          S.VEC,S.VALOF,
263          S.WHILE,
264          Ø
265
266      D("AND/*
267        *BE/BREAK/BY/*
268        *CASE/*
269        *DO/DEFAULT/*
270        *EQ/EQV/ELSE/ENDCASE/*
271        *FALSE/FOR/FINISH/*
272        *GOTO/GE/GR/GLOBAL/GET/*
273        *IF/INTO/*
274        *LET/LV/LE/LS/LOGOR/LOGAND/LOOP/LSHIFT//")
275
276      D("MANIFEST/*
277        *NE/NOT/NEQV/*
278        *OR/*
279        *RESULTIS/RETURN/REM/RSHIFT/RV/*
280        *REPEAT/REPEATWHILE/REPEATUNTIL/*
281        *SWITCHON/STATIC/*
282        *TO/TEST/TRUE/THEN/TABLE/*
283        *UNTIL/UNLESS/*
284        *VEC/VALOF/*
285        *WHILE/*
286        *$//")
287
288       NULLTAG := WORDNODE   $)1
289
290
291 AND D(WORDS) BE
292 $(1 LET I, LENGTH = 1, Ø
293
```

6.3   *Miscellaneous lexical analysis procedures*

Characters of raw source text are read by the routine RCH which assigns them to
the variable CH for the lexical analyser. It also implements the line-numbered
source-listing option as well as maintaining a circular buffer of the latest 64
characters of source that have been read. The content of this buffer is output
by WRCHBUF as part of any syntax error message generated by the routine
SYNREPORT described on page 102.

The routine RDTAG is used to read in the characters of identifiers, system words,
and section bracket tags and pack them into the vector WORDV, assigning to
WORDSIZE the subscript of the highest element of this vector that is used. The
formal parameter CHAR1 is used to hold the first character of the tag. For section
bracket tags, this character is a $ to eliminate any possible confusion with
identifiers and reserved words.

```
294     $( LET CH = GETBYTE(WORDS, I)
295        TEST CH='/'
296           THEN $( IF LENGTH=Ø RETURN
297                   CHARV!Ø := LENGTH
298                   WORDSIZE := PACKSTRING(CHARV, WORDV)
299                   LOOKUPWORD()
300                   H1!WORDNODE := !CODEP
301                   CODEP := CODEP + 1
302                   LENGTH := Ø  $)
303           ELSE $( LENGTH := LENGTH + 1
304                   CHARV!LENGTH := CH  $)
305        I := I + 1
306     $) REPEAT
307 $)1
308
309
310
311 .
312 //     LEX3
313
314 GET "SYNHDR"
315
316 LET RCH() BE
317     $( CH := RDCH()
318
319        IF PRSOURCE & GETP=Ø & CH NE ENDSTREAMCH DO
320           $( UNLESS LINECOUNT=PRLINE DO
321                          $( WRITEF("%I4  ", LINECOUNT)
322                             PRLINE := LINECOUNT  $)
323              WRCH(CH)  $)
324
325        CHCOUNT := CHCOUNT + 1
326        CHBUF!(CHCOUNT&63) := CH  $)
327
328 AND WRCHBUF() BE
329     $( WRITES ("*N..."),
330        FOR P = CHCOUNT-63 TO CHCOUNT DO
331                $( LET K = CHBUF!(P&63)
332                   UNLESS K=Ø DO WRCH(K)  $)
333        NEWLINE()  $)
334
335
336 AND RDTAG(CHAR1) BE
337     $( CHARP, CHARV!1 := 1, CHAR1
338
```

The routine PERFORMGET is called from NEXTSYMB to deal with the get-directive. It calls NEXTSYMB to read in the basic symbol following the word GET and a test is made to ensure that it is a string. Before selecting the new stream, it is necessary to save the current source stream, LINECOUNT and the value of CH in the next three words of the vector GETV. The get-stream is then opened and selected and its first character read. When this stream is eventually exhausted, the previously selected stream is reinstated by the code occurring near the end of the body of NEXTSYMB. One should note the natural way in which NEXTSYMB and PERFORMGET are mutually recursive.

Numerical constants are read in by a simple routine called READNUMBER. This expects the first digit of the number to be in CH and does the conversion for any base up to 16 as specified by the parameter RADIX. It uses an auxiliary function VALUE to convert each digit of the number into its binary value. Non-hexadecimal digits are given the artificially large value 100 so that the termination test in READNUMBER works correctly.

```
339              $( RCH()
340                 UNLESS 'A'<=CH<='Z' |
341                        'Ø'<=CH<='9' |
342                           CH='.' BREAK
343                 CHARP := CHARP+1
344                 CHARV!CHARP := CH  $) REPEAT
345
346              CHARV!Ø := CHARP
347              WORDSIZE := PACKSTRING(CHARV, WORDV)  $)
348
349
350 AND PERFORMGET() BE
351     $( NEXTSYMB()
352        UNLESS SYMB=S.STRING THEN SYNREPORT(97)
353
354        GETV!GETP := SOURCESTREAM
355        GETV!(GETP+1) := LINECOUNT
356        GETV!(GETP+2) := CH
357        GETP := GETP + 3
358        LINECOUNT := 1
359        SOURCESTREAM := FINDINPUT(WORDV)
360        IF SOURCESTREAM=Ø THEN SYNREPORT(96,WORDV)
361        SELECTINPUT(SOURCESTREAM)
362        RCH()    $)
363
364
365
366 AND READNUMBER(RADIX) BE
367     $( LET D = VALUE(CH)
368        DECVAL := D
369        IF D>=RADIX DO SYNREPORT(33)
370
371        $( RCH()
372           D := VALUE(CH)
373           IF D>=RADIX RETURN
374           DECVAL := RADIX*DECVAL + D  $) REPEAT
375     $)
376
377
378 AND VALUE(CH) = 'Ø'<=CH<='9' -> CH-'Ø',
379                 'A'<=CH<='F' -> CH-'A'+1Ø,
380                 1ØØ
381
```

Finally, the function RDSTRCH is used to read a single string character allowing for the escape conventions that are available in string and character constants.

6.4 The applicative expression tree

The result of syntax analysis is a tree structure called the *applicative expression tree* (or AE tree) which is an internal representation of the entire source program. Each node of the tree consists of a small number of consecutive words of store, the first of which always holds the integer code for an operator or keyword. The structure of the AE tree is given in table 6.1 in a BNF-like notation in which nodes are represented as lists of items enclosed in parentheses. The words that appear to

Table 6.1   The structure of the AE tree

```
E   ::=    NAME | (STRING, <packed characters>) |
           (NUMBER, <value>) | (TRUE) | (FALSE) |
           (VALOF, C) | (LV, E) | (RV, E) |
           (FNAP, E, E) | (FNAP, E, 0) | (MULT, E, E) |
           (DIV, E, E) | (REM, E, E) | (PLUS, E, E) |
           (MINUS, E, E) | (NEG, E) | (EQ, E, E) | (NE, E, E) |
           (LS, E, E) | (GR, E, E) | (LE, E, E) | (GE, E, E) |
           (NOT, E) | (LSHIFT, E, E) | (RSHIFT, E, E) |
           (LOGAND, E, E) | (LOGOR, E, E) | (EQV, E, E) | (NEQV, E, E) |
           (COND, E, E, E) | (TABLE, E) | (COMMA, E, E)

NAME ::= (NAME, −, <packed characters>)

C   ::=    (ASS, E, E) | (RTAP, E, E) | (RTAP, E, 0) |
           (GOTO, E) | (COLON, NAME, C, −) | (IF, E, C) |
           (UNLESS, E, C) | (WHILE, E, C) | (UNTIL, E, C) |
           (REPEAT, C) | (REPEATUNTIL, C, E) |
           (REPEATWHILE, C, E) | (TEST, E, C, C) | (BREAK) |
           (RETURN) | (FINISH) | (RESULTIS, E) |
           (FOR, NAME, E, E, 0, C) |
           (FOR, NAME, E, E, E, C) |
           (SWITCHON, E, C) | (CASE, E, C) | (ENDCASE) |
           (DEFAULT, C) | (LET, D, C) |
           (MANIFEST, CDEFS, C) | (STATIC, CDEFS, C) |
           (GLOBAL, CDEFS, C) | (SEQ, C, C) | 0

CDEFS ::= (CONSTDEF, CDEFS, NAME, E) | 0

D   ::=    (AND, D, D) | (VALDEF, NLIST, E) |
           (VECDEF, NAME, E) | (FNDEF, NAME, FPL, E, −) |
           (RTDEF, NAME, FPL, C. −)

NLIST ::= (COMMA, NAME, NLIST) | NAME

FPL ::= NLIST | 0
```

```
382 AND RDSTRCH( ) = VALOF
383 $(1 LET K = CH
384
385     RCH( )
386
387     IF K='*N' DO SYNREPORT(34)
388
389     IF K='**' DO
390         $( IF CH='*N' | CH='*S' | CH='*T' DO
391             $( $( IF CH='*N' DO LINECOUNT := LINECOUNT+1
392                 RCH( )
393               $) REPEATWHILE CH='*N' | CH='*S' | CH='*T'
394               UNLESS CH='**' DO SYNREPORT(34)
395               RCH( )
396               RESULTIS RDSTRCH( )
397             $)
398
399             K := CH
400             IF CH='T' DO K := '*T'
401             IF CH='S' DO K := '*S'
402             IF CH='N' DO K := '*N'
403             IF CH='B' DO K := '*B'
404             IF CH='P' DO K := '*P'
405             RCH( )  $)
406
407     RESULTIS K  $)1
408 .
409 //    SYNØ
410
411 GET "SYNHDR"
412
413 LET NEWVEC(N) = VALOF
414     $( TREEP := TREEP - N - 1
415         IF TREEP<=TREEVEC DO
416                 $( REPORTMAX := Ø
417                     SYNREPORT(98)  $)
418         RESULTIS TREEP  $)
419
420 AND LIST1(X) = VALOF
421     $( LET P = NEWVEC(Ø)
422         P!Ø := X
423         RESULTIS P  $)
```

the left of :: = are analogous to syntactic categories and represent pointers to nodes in the AE tree. All other words appearing in the syntax denote the integer codes for the types of the nodes. In string and name nodes, the packed characters occupy as many computer words as they need. The value in a number node occupies one word. As a general rule, the AE tree structure can be derived from the BCPL syntax by taking each syntactic construction in turn, selecting a suitable keyword or operator to distinguish it and laying out the operands in the same order in which they appear in the source program. For instance, the command

```
TEST E THEN C1 ELSE C2
```

has the corresponding AE tree structure

(TEST, E, C1, C2)

Elements of nodes which are used as working space in the translation phase or which are list pointers in name nodes are indicated by dashes.

The syntax analysis is performed by the method of recursive descent, and since this process involves no backtracking it is possible to use a very simple scheme for the allocation of space used by AE tree nodes. Space for these nodes is taken from the vector called TREEVEC under the control of a pointer TREEP which initially points to its last word. Whenever a new node is required, the function NEWVEC is called with a parameter giving the node's size. NEWVEC decrements TREEP by the appropriate amount, checks that there is still space left and then returns with a pointer to the node obtained. The only nodes of variable size are those for identifiers and string constants, and these are constructed using NEWVEC directly. The size of every other node depends only on its type and is conveniently constructed with the aid of one of the functions from LIST1 to LIST6 which take from one to six arguments respectively, specifying the element values of the created node.

FORMTREE is the main function of the syntax analyser and, as such, its job is to initialise several variables and data structures that are used during syntax analysis. It starts by initialising the character input interface by allocating space for the circular buffer CHBUF, initialising certain counts and making the first call of RCH. If the input stream is exhausted at this stage, FORMTREE returns a value zero to the steering program to indicate that there are no more sections of source code to be compiled. Space is allocated for the vector GETV for use by PERFORMGET for the implementation of the get-directive. The vectors WORDV and CHARV are then allocated for use by NEXTSYMB and LOOKUPWORD for the analysis of variable length symbols. Finally the name table is allocated and initialised with entries for all the reserved words with the aid of DECLSYSWORDS as described above.

```
424
425 AND LIST2(X, Y) = VALOF
426     $( LET P = NEWVEC(1)
427        P!Ø, P!1 := X, Y
428        RESULTIS P    $)
429
43Ø AND LIST3(X, Y, Z) = VALOF
431    $( LET P = NEWVEC(2)
432       P!Ø, P!1, P!2 := X, Y, Z
433       RESULTIS P       $)
434
435 AND LIST4(X, Y, Z, T) = VALOF
436    $( LET P = NEWVEC(3)
437       P!Ø, P!1, P!2, P!3 := X, Y, Z, T
438       RESULTIS P    $)
439
44Ø AND LIST5(X, Y, Z, T, U) = VALOF
441    $( LET P = NEWVEC(4)
442       P!Ø, P!1, P!2, P!3, P!4 := X, Y, Z, T, U
443       RESULTIS P    $)
444
445 AND LIST6(X, Y, Z, T, U, V) = VALOF
446    $( LET P = NEWVEC(5)
447       P!Ø, P!1, P!2, P!3, P!4, P!5 := X, Y, Z, T, U, V
448       RESULTIS P $)
449
45Ø AND FORMTREE() =  VALOF
451 $(1 LET V = VEC 63
452     CHBUF := V
453     FOR I = Ø TO 63 DO CHBUF!I := Ø
454     CHCOUNT := Ø
455     LINECOUNT, PRLINE := 1, Ø
456     RCH()
457     IF CH=ENDSTREAMCH RESULTIS Ø
458
459  $( LET V = VEC 2Ø   // for get-streams
46Ø     GETV, GETP, GETT := V, Ø, 2Ø
461
462 $( LET V = VEC 128
463     WORDV := V
464
465 $( LET V = VEC 256
466     CHARV, CHARP := V, Ø
```

The variables REC.P and REC.L are used in SYNREPORT in the code dealing with the recovery after syntax errors. They must therefore be initialised before the first call of NEXTSYMB. At this point there is a compiler debugging option built into the program to assist implementers who are bootstrapping the compiler. It is controlled by OPTION!1 which is set by the steering program. When it is set, the compiler does not perform syntax analysis but executes a simple loop that prints the integer code for each basic symbol of the source program together with the characters held in WORDV. A section of BCPL program is syntactically equivalent to a block body and so is read by the function RDBLOCKBODY described later.

FORMTREE is typical of a kind of function, which occurs quite often in large BCPL programs, to initialise variables and allocate workspace before calling the procedure that does the work. Such a sequence of initialising statements is structurally simple but none-the-less important since forgetting to initialise a variable can lead to obscure runtime errors. Using tagged section brackets to close more than one section is not normally recommended, but the use of $)1 at the end of FORMTREE to close six sections is perfectly satisfactory since the logical structure of this function is so simple.

When a syntactic error is detected, the routine SYNREPORT is called with an integer argument specifying the nature of the error. This routine prints a suitable message giving the approximate line number of the error and the current contents of the circular buffer. Unless too many errors have already been detected, SYNREPORT tries to resume syntax analysis at a sensible place. It first reads in basic symbols until the end of the current line is reached, or LET, AND or a section bracket is found, and then makes a non-local jump by the call LONGJUMP(·REC.P, REC.L) to the current recovery point.

```
467
468   $( LET V = VEC NAMETABLESIZE
469      NAMETABLE := V
470      FOR I = Ø TO NAMETABLESIZE DO NAMETABLE!I :=   Ø
471      DECLSYSWORDS()
472
473      REC.P, REC.L := LEVEL(), L
474
475   L: NEXTSYMB()
476
477      IF OPTION!1 DO   //   LEX debugging option
478          $( WRITEF("%I3 %S*N", SYMB, WORDV)
479              IF SYMB=S.END RESULTIS Ø
480              GOTO L  $)
481
482   $( LET A = RDBLOCKBODY()
483      UNLESS SYMB=S.END DO SYNREPORT(99)
484
485      RESULTIS A          $)1
486
487
488
489 AND SYNREPORT(N, A) BE
490 $( REPORTCOUNT := REPORTCOUNT + 1
491    WRITEF ("*NSYNTAX ERROR NEAR LINE %N: ", LINECOUNT)
492    SYNMESSAGE(N, A)
493    WRCHBUF()
494    IF REPORTCOUNT GR REPORTMAX DO
495              $( WRITES("*NCOMPILATION ABORTED*N")
496                STOP(8)   $)
497    NLPENDING := FALSE
498
499    UNTIL SYMB=S.LSECT | SYMB=S.RSECT |
500         SYMB=S.LET | SYMB=S.AND |
501         SYMB=S.END | NLPENDING DO NEXTSYMB()
502    LONGJUMP(REC.P, REC.L)   $)
503
504 AND SYNMESSAGE(N, A) BE
505 $( LET S = VALOF SWITCHON N INTO
506     $( DEFAULT:  A := N; RESULTIS "ERROR %N"
507
```

(This page has no text.)

```
508       CASE 91: RESULTIS "'$' OUT OF CONTEXT"
509       CASE 94: RESULTIS "ILLEGAL CHARACTER"
510       CASE 96: RESULTIS "NO INPUT %S"
511       CASE 97: RESULTIS "BAD GET DIRECTIVE"
512       CASE 98: RESULTIS "PROGRAM TOO LARGE"
513       CASE 99: RESULTIS "INCORRECT TERMINATION"
514
515       CASE 8:CASE 40:CASE 43:
516               RESULTIS "NAME EXPECTED"
517       CASE 6:  RESULTIS "'$(' EXPECTED"
518       CASE 7:  RESULTIS "'$)' EXPECTED"
519       CASE 9:  RESULTIS "UNTAGGED '$)' MISMATCH"
520       CASE 32: RESULTIS "ERROR IN EXPRESSION"
521       CASE 33: RESULTIS "BAD NUMBER"
522       CASE 34: RESULTIS "BAD STRING OR CHARACTER CONSTANT"
523       CASE 15:CASE 19:CASE 41: RESULTIS "')' MISSING"
524       CASE 30: RESULTIS "BAD CONDITIONAL EXPRESSION"
525       CASE 42: RESULTIS "BAD PROCEDURE HEADING"
526       CASE 44:
527       CASE 45: RESULTIS "BAD DECLARATION"
528       CASE 50: RESULTIS "UNEXPECTED ':'"
529       CASE 51: RESULTIS "ERROR IN COMMAND"
530       CASE 54: RESULTIS "'ELSE' EXPECTED"
531       CASE 57:
532       CASE 58: RESULTIS "BAD FOR-LOOP"
533       CASE 60: RESULTIS "'INTO' EXPECTED"
534       CASE 61:CASE 62: RESULTIS "':' EXPECTED"
535       CASE 63: RESULTIS "'**/' MISSING"
536    $)
537
538 WRITEF(S, A)  $)
539
540
541 .
542 //     SYN1
543
544 GET "SYNHDR"
545
546 LET RDBLOCKBODY() = VALOF
547 $(1 LET P, L = REC.P, REC.L
548     LET A = 0
549
```

6.5 RDBLOCKBODY, RDSEQ, RDCDEFS, *and* RDSECT

RDBLOCKBODY is the function which performs the analysis of the body of a block or compound command and yields the corresponding AE tree representation. A block body is basically a command sequence, possibly preceded by a sequence of declarations. The kind of a declaration can be determined from its first symbol. If it is MANIFEST, STATIC or GLOBAL, then the body of the declaration is enclosed in section brackets and is read by the call RDSECT(RDCDEFS). The function RDSECT deals with the matching of section brackets, and RDCDEFS is a function which will read a sequence of constant definitions of the form

<name>=E   or   <name>:E

Having read the declaration, the block body is read by a call of RDBLOCKBODY and the appropriate node constructed.

A let-declaration consists of the word LET followed by a sequence of definitions connected by ANDs. The definitions are read by repeated calls of RDEF while SYMB has the value S.AND. The rest of the block body is read by a call of RDBLOCKBODY.

The command labelled RECOVER is the main recovery point after syntactic errors. This label and the current stack pointer (obtained by a call for LEVEL) are assigned to the global variables REC.L and REC.P for use by SYNREPORT. The old values of REC.P and REC.L are saved and restored appropriately.

If the block body does not start with a declaration, then it must be a command sequence and this is read by a call for RDSEQ. Since semicolons are only necessary to separate commands which would otherwise elide, they may often be omitted and thus the end of a sequence must be detected by the presence of a closing section bracket or symbol S.END rather than by the absence of a semicolon. The call IGNORE(S.SEMICOLON) ignores semicolons by calling NEXTSYMB if the current symbol is a semicolon. The commands of the sequence are read in by calls for RCOM.

```
55Ø     REC.P, REC.L := LEVEL(), RECOVER
551
552     IGNORE(S.SEMICOLON)
553
554     SWITCHON SYMB INTO
555     $(S CASE S.MANIFEST:
556         CASE S.STATIC:
557         CASE S.GLOBAL:
558             $(  LET OP = SYMB
559                 NEXTSYMB()
56Ø                 A := RDSECT(RDCDEFS)
561                 A := LIST3(OP, A, RDBLOCKBODY())
562                 ENDCASE  $)
563
564
565         CASE S.LET: NEXTSYMB()
566                     A := RDEF()
567           RECOVER: WHILE SYMB=S.AND DO
568                        $( NEXTSYMB()
569                           A := LIST3(S.AND, A, RDEF()) $)
57Ø                     A := LIST3(S.LET, A, RDBLOCKBODY())
571                     ENDCASE
572
573         DEFAULT: A := RDSEQ()
574
575                 UNLESS SYMB=S.RSECT | SYMB=S.END DO
576                         SYNREPORT(51)
577
578         CASE S.RSECT: CASE S.END:
579     $)S
58Ø
581     REC.P, REC.L := P, L
582     RESULTIS A    $)1
583
584 AND RDSEQ() = VALOF
585     $( LET A = Ø
586        IGNORE(S.SEMICOLON)
587        A := RCOM()
588        IF SYMB=S.RSECT | SYMB=S.END RESULTIS A
589        RESULTIS LIST3(S.SEQ, A, RDSEQ())   $)
59Ø
591
```

The BCPL rule concerning the automatic insertion of closing section brackets is implemented by the function RDSECT. When RDSECT is called the current symbol is an opening section bracket whose tag is in a tree node pointed to by WORDNODE. This pointer is held in the local variable TAG for later comparison with the tag of the closing bracket. The parameter of RDSECT is a function to analyse the text between the section brackets. This function will be RDBLOCKBODY, RDCDEFS or RDSEQ. These functions should read until a closing section bracket is reached. RDSECT checks for the closing bracket and if one is not found a report is generated. Its tag is then compared with the tag of the opening section bracket and NEXTSYMB called if they match. If the tags do not match and if the closing bracket has a null tag then an error is reported. Notice that, if the tags do not match and the closing bracket is not null, then NEXTSYMB is not called, leaving SYMB containing the closing section bracket. This, in effect, inserts an appropriate closing section bracket for the current level.

The function RNAME is called when a name is expected; it first checks that the current symbol is a name and then yields as result the value of WORDNODE which will have been set by the call of LOOKUPWORD in the lexical analyser. One should note that all occurrences of the same name yield pointers to the same node. This simplifies name comparison in the translation phase of the compiler.

RNAMELIST is a function that reads a list of names separated by commas.

IGNORE and CHECKFOR are routines that are used to facilitate the treatment of delimiter symbols.

```
592 AND RDCDEFS() = VALOF
593 $(1 LET A, B = Ø, Ø
594     LET PTR = ∂A
595     LET P, L = REC.P, REC.L
596     REC.P, REC.L := LEVEL(), REC
597
598     $( B := RNAME()
599         TEST SYMB=S.EQ | SYMB=S.COLON THEN NEXTSYMB()
600                                       ELSE SYNREPORT(45)
601         !PTR := LIST4(S.CONSTDEF, Ø, B, REXP(Ø))
602         PTR := ∂H2!(!PTR)
603  REC: IGNORE(S.SEMICOLON) $) REPEATWHILE SYMB=S.NAME
604
605     REC.P, REC.L := P, L
606     RESULTIS A  $)1
607
608 AND RDSECT(R) = VALOF
609     $( LET TAG, A = WORDNODE, Ø
610         CHECKFOR(S.LSECT, 6)
611         A := R()
612         UNLESS SYMB=S.RSECT DO SYNREPORT(7)
613         TEST TAG=WORDNODE
614             THEN NEXTSYMB()
615             ELSE IF WORDNODE=NULLTAG DO
616                     $( SYMB := Ø
617                         SYNREPORT(9)  $)
618         RESULTIS A   $)
619
620
621 AND RNAMELIST() = VALOF
622     $( LET A = RNAME()
623         UNLESS SYMB=S.COMMA RESULTIS A
624         NEXTSYMB()
625         RESULTIS LIST3(S.COMMA, A, RNAMELIST())  $)
626
627
628 AND RNAME() = VALOF
629     $( LET A = WORDNODE
630         CHECKFOR(S.NAME, 8)
631         RESULTIS A  $)
632
633 AND IGNORE(ITEM) BE IF SYMB=ITEM DO NEXTSYMB()
634
```

6.6   The analysis of expressions

Expressions are composed of basic expressions connected by infixed operators. They are parsed by the two functions RBEXP and REXP. RBEXP reads a basic expression and yields as result its AE tree form, and REXP reads a general expression and is primarily concerned with the parsing of infixed operators. Both RBEXP and REXP are called with the first symbol of the expression in SYMB and on exit SYMB contains the first symbol following the expression read.

   RBEXP switches on SYMB to determine which kind of basic expression is present and an error message is generated if SYMB cannot start an expression. If the current symbol is TRUE, FALSE, or a name, then the node pointed to by WORDNODE is the AE tree representation of the basic expression. If the current symbol is a string, then a node is obtained by a call for NEWVEC and the string copied into it. The number of words required to hold the string was computed when the lexical analyser packed the string and it was left in WORDSIZE. If the current symbol is a number, then a suitable number node is constructed using the value in DECVAL. A left parenthesis introduces a bracketed expression. The enclosed expression is read by the call REXP(∅) and then the matching parenthesis is checked. The body of a valof-expression is a command and this is read by a call for RCOM. The remaining cases in RBEXP are monadic expression operators of various binding powers. The operands are read in by suitable calls of REXP. If the operand of monadic minus is a number then its numerical value is negated.

```
635 AND CHECKFOR(ITEM, N) BE
636         $( UNLESS SYMB=ITEM DO SYNREPORT(N)
637             NEXTSYMB()  $)
638
639 .
640 //     SYN2
641
642 GET "SYNHDR"
643
644 LET RBEXP() = VALOF
645 $(1 LET A, OP = Ø, SYMB
646
647      SWITCHON SYMB INTO
648
649  $( DEFAULT: SYNREPORT(32)
650
651     CASE S.TRUE:
652     CASE S.FALSE:
653     CASE S.NAME:
654         A := WORDNODE
655         NEXTSYMB()
656         RESULTIS A
657
658     CASE S.STRING:
659         A := NEWVEC(WORDSIZE+1)
660         A!Ø := S.STRING
661         FOR I = Ø TO WORDSIZE DO A!(I+1) := WORDV!I
662         NEXTSYMB()
663         RESULTIS A
664
665     CASE S.NUMBER:
666         A := LIST2(S.NUMBER, DECVAL)
667         NEXTSYMB()
668         RESULTIS A
669
670     CASE S.LPAREN:
671         NEXTSYMB()
672         A := REXP(Ø)
673         CHECKFOR(S.RPAREN, 15)
674         RESULTIS A
675
676     CASE S.VALOF:
677         NEXTSYMB()
678         RESULTIS LIST2(S.VALOF, RCOM()))
```

REXP is the function that parses a general arithmetic expression. The left- and right-hand precedence of operators control the analysis. The right-hand operand of any operator is read by a call for REXP with the operator's right-hand precedence as argument. On entry, it uses RBEXP to read the basic expression that starts the general expression and then switches on the symbol that follows. If this symbol is not an infixed operator, then the entire expression has been read and REXP returns. If the symbol is a left parenthesis then a function application has been encountered and it is parsed by reading in the actual parameters, if any, and then checking for the right parenthesis. Every other infixed operator has its left precedence checked with the formal parameter of REXP to determine whether it may be incorporated into the result. If the test succeeds, then the right-hand operand is read by a call of REXP using the operator's right-hand precedence. Within the program the operator's left and right precedence values are usually held in the local variables P and Q respectively and the parsing is performed by the statements labelled DYADIC on line 759.

N is the formal parameter of REXP, OP is the operator and A is a local variable which holds the AE tree form of the expression to the left of the operator. For left associative operators, the left and right precedences are equal; such operators are parsed by setting P and then jumping to LASSOC where Q is set equal to P before executing the statement labelled DYADIC. After reading the right hand operand and constructing a suitable tree node, REXP executes the switch again and the process is repeated until either there are no more infixed operators or one is encountered with insufficient left precedence.

```
679
68Ø     CASE S.VECAP: OP := S.RV
681     CASE S.LV:
682     CASE S.RV: NEXTSYMB(); RESULTIS LIST2(OP, REXP(35))
683
684     CASE S.PLUS: NEXTSYMB(); RESULTIS REXP(34)
685
686     CASE S.MINUS: NEXTSYMB()
687                   A := REXP(34)
688                   TEST H1!A=S.NUMBER
689                       THEN H2!A := - H2!A
69Ø                       ELSE A := LIST2(S.NEG, A)
691                   RESULTIS A
692
693     CASE S.NOT: NEXTSYMB()
694                 RESULTIS LIST2(S.NOT, REXP(24))
695
696     CASE S.TABLE:NEXTSYMB()
697                  RESULTIS LIST2(S.TABLE, REXPLIST())    $)1
698
699
7ØØ AND REXP(N) = VALOF
7Ø1 $(1 LET A = RBEXP()
7Ø2
7Ø3     LET B, C, P, Q = Ø, Ø, Ø, Ø
7Ø4
7Ø5 $(2 LET OP = SYMB
7Ø6
7Ø7     IF NLPENDING RESULTIS A
7Ø8
7Ø9     SWITCHON OP INTO
71Ø $(S
711 DEFAULT: RESULTIS A
712
713 CASE S.LPAREN: NEXTSYMB()
714                B := Ø
715                UNLESS SYMB=S.RPAREN DO B := REXPLIST()
716                CHECKFOR(S.RPAREN, 19)
717                A := LIST3(S.FNAP, A, B)
718                LOOP
719
```

The parsing of relational operators is special since they are non-associative and since the logical operator 'and' needs to be inserted between the individual relations of an extended relation. The conditional expression is also exceptional since it has two right-hand operands separated by a comma.

BCPL allows the programmer to omit the semicolons that separate commands in most instances and, in particular, between commands which are on different lines. To ensure that this will always work, the language states that a dyadic operator may not be the first symbol of a line. This is implemented by inspecting NLPENDING before executing the switch in REXP. NLPENDING is set in NEXTSYMB as described above.

```
720 CASE S.VECAP: P := 40; GOTO LASSOC
721
722 CASE S.REM:CASE S.MULT:CASE S.DIV: P := 35; GOTO LASSOC
723
724 CASE S.PLUS:CASE S.MINUS: P := 34; GOTO LASSOC
725
726 CASE S.EQ:CASE S.NE:
727 CASE S.LE:CASE S.GE:
728 CASE S.LS:CASE S.GR:
729     IF N>=30 RESULTIS A
730
731     $(R NEXTSYMB()
732         B := REXP(30)
733         A := LIST3(OP, A, B)
734         TEST C=0 THEN C :=   A
735                     ELSE C := LIST3(S.LOGAND, C, A)
736         A, OP := B, SYMB  $)R REPEATWHILE S.EQ<=OP<=S.GE
737
738     A := C
739     LOOP
740
741 CASE S.LSHIFT:CASE S.RSHIFT: P, Q := 25, 30; GOTO DYADIC
742
743 CASE S.LOGAND: P := 23; GOTO LASSOC
744
745 CASE S.LOGOR:  P := 22; GOTO LASSOC
746
747 CASE S.EQV:CASE S.NEQV: P := 21; GOTO LASSOC
748
749 CASE S.COND:
750         IF N>=13 RESULTIS A
751         NEXTSYMB()
752         B := REXP(0)
753         CHECKFOR(S.COMMA, 30)
754         A := LIST4(S.COND, A, B, REXP(0))
755         LOOP
756
757 LASSOC: Q := P
758
759 DYADIC: IF N>=P RESULTIS A
```

6.7   The analysis of definitions

The function RDEF is called after encountering the basic symbol LET or AND to
read the definition. There are four forms of definition in BCPL: function
definitions, routine definitions, simple definitions and vector definitions. They all
start with a name, and a simple definition may start with a name list. The name or
name list is read in by a call for RNAMELIST and its tree form held in the local
variable N. The symbol that follows should either be a left parenthesis indicating
the presence of a function or routine definition or an equals sign indicating a
simple or vector definition.

For a function or routine definition, a check is made to ensure that N is a name
(not a name list) and then the formal parameter list is read. The defining operator,
which should be either the word BE or an equals sign, distinguishes between the
two possible kinds of definition.

The body of a routine is a command read by RCOM and the body of a function is
an expression read by REXP. The fifth element of the AE node for function and
routine definitions is working space used by the next stage of the compiler.

Simple and vector definitions are distinguished by the symbol that follows the
equals sign. If it is VEC then a vector definition has been encountered, and it is
necessary to check that N is a name.

```
760                    NEXTSYMB()
761                    A := LIST3(OP, A, REXP(Q))
762                    LOOP
763 $)S
764 $)2 REPEAT
765 $)1
766
767 LET REXPLIST() = VALOF
768      $(1 LET A = Ø
769          LET PTR = ðA
77Ø
771          $( LET B = REXP(Ø)
772             UNLESS SYMB=S.COMMA DO $( !PTR := B
773                                       RESULTIS A  $)
774             NEXTSYMB()
775             !PTR := LIST3(S.COMMA, B, Ø)
776             PTR := ðH3!(!PTR)  $) REPEAT
777      $)1
778
779 LET RDEF() = VALOF
78Ø $(1 LET N = RNAMELIST()
781
782      SWITCHON SYMB INTO
783
784  $( CASE S.LPAREN:
785  $( LET A = Ø
786     NEXTSYMB()
787     UNLESS H1!N=S.NAME DO SYNREPORT(4Ø)
788     IF SYMB=S.NAME DO A := RNAMELIST()
789     CHECKFOR(S.RPAREN, 41)
79Ø
791     IF SYMB=S.BE DO
792        $( NEXTSYMB()
793           RESULTIS LIST5(S.RTDEF, N, A, RCOM(), Ø) $)
794
795     IF SYMB=S.EQ DO
796        $( NEXTSYMB()
797           RESULTIS LIST5(S.FNDEF, N, A, REXP(Ø), Ø) $)
798
799     SYNREPORT(42)  $)
8ØØ
```

6.8   The analysis of commands

Commands are parsed by the functions RBCOM and RCOM. The process used is
similar to that used in the parsing of expressions, only, since there are so few
infixed command operators, it is not necessary to use precedence. RBCOM parses
basic commands and RCOM analyses general commands.

The kind of basic command is determined by its first symbol in all but three
cases, which are assignments, routine commands and labelled commands. These
three can be distinguished by reading in an expression and then looking at the
symbol that follows. If it is the assignment operator, then the right-hand side is
read and an assignment node is constructed. If the symbol is a colon, a check is
made to ensure that the expression read was a name and then a labelled-command
node is constructed. The fourth element in this node is used as working space by
the next phase of the compiler. If the symbol is anything else, then a routine
command must have been encountered. It would have been parsed as a function
application by REXP; the node is checked and, if correct, is converted into a
routine application node.

```
8Ø1  DEFAULT: SYNREPORT(44)
8Ø2
8Ø3  CASE S.EQ:
8Ø4       NEXTSYMB()
8Ø5        IF SYMB=S.VEC DO
8Ø6             $( NEXTSYMB()
8Ø7                 UNLESS H1!N=S.NAME DO SYNREPORT(43)
8Ø8                 RESULTIS LIST3(S.VECDEF, N, REXP(Ø))  $)
8Ø9             RESULTIS LIST3(S.VALDEF, N, REXPLIST())
81Ø  $)  $)1
811  .
812  //    SYN4
813
814  GET "SYNHDR"
815
816  LET RBCOM() = VALOF
817  $(1 LET A, B, OP = Ø, Ø, SYMB
818
819      SWITCHON SYMB INTO
82Ø   $( DEFAULT: RESULTIS Ø
821
822      CASE S.NAME:CASE S.NUMBER:CASE S.STRING:
823      CASE S.TRUE:CASE S.FALSE:
825      CASE S.LV:CASE S.RV:CASE S.VECAP:
825      CASE S.LPAREN:
826             A := REXPLIST()
827
828             IF SYMB=S.ASS  THEN
829                $( OP := SYMB
83Ø                   NEXTSYMB()
831                   RESULTIS LIST3(OP, A, REXPLIST())  $)
832
833             IF SYMB=S.COLON THEN
834                $( UNLESS H1!A=S.NAME DO SYNREPORT(5Ø)
835                   NEXTSYMB()
836                   RESULTIS LIST4(S.COLON, A, RBCOM(), Ø)  $)
837
838             IF H1!A=S.FNAP THEN
839                 $( H1!A := S.RTAP
84Ø                    RESULTIS A  $)
841
```

All other forms of command are determined by the first symbol and they are parsed in a straightforward way. Delimiting symbols which must be present are checked by suitable calls of CHECKFOR and the optional occurrences of DO are dealt with by the call IGNORE(S.DO). If the command starts with a section bracket then it is a block or compound command, and is read by a call for RDSECT which implements the section bracket tagging rule. Its argument RDBLOCKBODY is a function which reads the text between the section brackets. The AE form of the basic commands LOOP, BREAK, ENDCASE, FINISH, and RETURN is the node in the name tree pointed to by WORDNODE.

```
842                  SYNREPORT(51)
843                  RESULTIS A
844
845     CASE S.GOTO:CASE S.RESULTIS:
846                  NEXTSYMB()
847                  RESULTIS LIST2(OP, REXP(Ø))
848
849     CASE S.IF:CASE S.UNLESS:
85Ø     CASE S.WHILE:CASE S.UNTIL:
851                  NEXTSYMB()
852                  A := REXP(Ø)
853                  IGNORE(S.DO)
854                  RESULTIS LIST3(OP, A, RCOM())
855
856     CASE S.TEST:
857                  NEXTSYMB()
858                  A := REXP(Ø)
859                  IGNORE(S.DO)
86Ø                  B := RCOM()
861                  CHECKFOR(S.OR, 54)
862                  RESULTIS LIST4(S.TEST, A, B, RCOM())
863
864     CASE S.FOR:
865      $(  LET I, J, K = Ø, Ø, Ø
866              NEXTSYMB()
867              A := RNAME()
868              CHECKFOR(S.EQ, 57)
869              I := REXP(Ø)
87Ø              CHECKFOR(S.TO, 58)
871              J := REXP(Ø)
872              IF SYMB=S.BY DO $( NEXTSYMB()
873                                 K := REXP(Ø)  $)
874              IGNORE(S.DO)
875              RESULTIS LIST6(S.FOR, A, I, J, K, RCOM())  $)
876
877     CASE S.LOOP:CASE S.BREAK:
878     CASE S.RETURN:CASE S.FINISH:CASE S.ENDCASE:
879              A := WORDNODE
88Ø              NEXTSYMB()
881              RESULTIS A
882
```

RCOM uses RBCOM to read the basic command; it then checks for occurrences of REPEAT, REPEATWHILE and REPEATUNTIL and constructs suitable repeat nodes as necessary. RBCOM is prepared to read an empty command, but RCOM checks that the command is not null. Empty commands may only appear after labels.

Exercises

1. List all the changes needed to the syntax analyser described in this chapter in order to deal with a new operator called ABS whose precedence is the same as monadic minus, and also the operator % described in section 4.9.

2. List the changes needed to implement the field-selector extension described in section 4.8.

3. List the changes that would be necessary to implement operators of the form <op>:= where <op> may be any dyadic arithmetic or bit-pattern operator. No space is permitted between <op> and :=. These new operators should behave syntactically just like :=.

```
883        CASE S.SWITCHON:
884                NEXTSYMB()
885                A := REXP(Ø)
886                CHECKFOR(S.INTO, 6Ø)
887                RESULTIS LIST3(S.SWITCHON, A, RDSECT(RDSEQ))
888
889        CASE S.CASE:
89Ø                NEXTSYMB()
891                A := REXP(Ø)
892                CHECKFOR(S.COLON, 61)
893                RESULTIS LIST3(S.CASE, A, RBCOM())
894
895        CASE S.DEFAULT:
896                NEXTSYMB()
897                CHECKFOR(S.COLON, 62)
898                RESULTIS LIST2(S.DEFAULT, RBCOM())
899
9ØØ        CASE S.LSECT:
9Ø1                RESULTIS RDSECT(RDBLOCKBODY)
9Ø2 $)1
9Ø3
9Ø4 AND RCOM() = VALOF
9Ø5 $(1 LET A = RBCOM()
9Ø6
9Ø7     IF A=Ø DO SYNREPORT(51)
9Ø8
9Ø9     WHILE SYMB=S.REPEAT | SYMB=S.REPEATWHILE |
91Ø                         SYMB=S.REPEATUNTIL DO
911             $( LET OP = SYMB
912                 NEXTSYMB()
913                 TEST OP=S.REPEAT
914                     THEN A := LIST2(OP, A)
915                     ELSE A := LIST3(OP, A, REXP(Ø))  $)
916
917     RESULTIS A
918 $)1
```

7
Compiler portability

7.1 Introduction

It is possible to construct a portable program in various ways by using, for instance, a standard language such as Fortran, or by writing the program in some suitable macro language. Another approach that is sometimes worthwhile is to use a non-standard but particularly suitable language, even though this may mean transferring its compiler to the target machine before transferring the application program. At first sight this seems to be an expensive way to proceed, but there are compensating advantages. For instance, compared with a macro code, a high-level language is, in general, easier to program since its syntax can be less restrictive and it can gain greater linguistic power by greater use of syntactic and semantic context. A compiler is usually able to generate code several times faster than a macro generator and this is important if the application program is large and if much rewriting or continued program development is expected on the target machine. The efficiency of the object code generated by a compiler is often better than that produced by macro generators, and the intelligibility of diagnostics messages can also be better.

A compiler is inherently a machine-dependent program since the part of it concerned with code generation must be rewritten for every different machine. A compiler also tends to be large, and large programs by their nature are less portable than small ones. However, if the language and its compiler are both designed with care, the work involved to transfer the implementation from one machine to another can be minimised. Such portability considerations have had a strong influence on the design of BCPL and its compiler.

While the code generation part of a compiler is machine dependent, the rest can be written in such a way that only minimal changes are required when moving it to a new machine. It is normal to separate the machine dependent and independent parts so that the changes can be localised in a smaller area. To achieve this, the BCPL compiler is structured as in figure 7.1, where the syntactic phase is largely machine independent while the code generator is not.

The choice of a suitable intermediate form was one of the key decisions in the design of the compiler since it affected the level of portability and efficiency obtainable. Many significantly different forms of interface were considered. It

124

Fig. 7.1   The structure of the BCPL compiler

could have been either a set of procedure calls for the syntactic phase to make on the code generator, or a data structure (such as a parse tree) to be handed to the code generator for compilation, or a partially compiled translation of the program in the form of a linear sequence of statements in some intermediate object code. The choice is, of course, a compromise. On the one hand, an intermediate code might have been chosen that was reasonably close to the machine language of a typical target computer, in which case the code generation would be relatively simple since most of the translation decisions would by that time have been made. Alternatively, the interface could have been much closer to the original source language giving the code generator much greater scope for global and local optimisation.

One important consideration is that the transporting process is usually based on the interface code and so one must ensure that it can be written to magnetic tape and read without undue difficulty. Bearing in mind the immense difficulty that people often experience with tape when transferring alphanumeric card images, one should not underestimate the difficulty of transferring anything more complicated (such as re-entrant list structures of mixed binary and character data). One should also remember that the installer is usually far less familiar with the compiler design and its intermediate code than the donor of the system. Indeed the installer may spend more time trying to understand the compiler and the interface than the time he eventually needs to write a code generator.

In practice the interface in most existing portable compilers is usually in the form of a linear sequence of simple statements in some intermediate code specifically designed for each language, even though greater compiled code efficiency can be obtained by using a more structured interface.

7.2   OCODE

The intermediate form for BCPL is called OCODE, and follows this pattern. It is described in full in Richards [11]. It can be regarded as the assembly language of a simple abstract machine for BCPL. This machine has a store for variables consisting of equal-sized cells which can be addressed using integers in such a way that consecutive integers refer to adjacent cells. This store is subdivided into three areas: a vector for global variables; an area for static variables; and the stack for local variables, arguments and anonymous results. The machine contains two registers used for addressing: G which points to the base of the global vector; and P which points to the region of stack belonging to the currently active procedure.

To aid description, there is a variable S which holds the size of the current stack frame. Its value varies dynamically during execution as blocks are entered and left, but no central register need be provided for it since its value is always known at every point in the program. Many of the basic operations in the machine are concerned with loading, storing or modifying values on or near the top of the stack, and we will use P!(S-1) and P!(S-2) to denote the top two locations of the current stack frame. This notation is shown pictorially in figure 7.2.

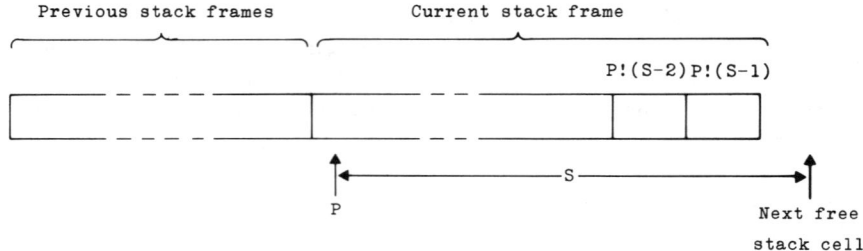

Fig. 7.2   The runtime stack

Static variables are allocated storage cells that are addressed by internal symbolic labels of the form Ln where n is an integer.

An OCODE statement consists of a keyword identifying the statement followed by a variable number of simple arguments. Most of these statements are semantically weak but sequences of them can easily be used to form the reverse Polish translation of a BCPL program.

Access to local variables is provided by three statements which can be specified as follows:

```
LP  n   means  S:=S+1; P!(S-1):=P!n
LLP n   means  S:=S+1; P!(S-1):=P+n
SP  n   means  P!n:=P!(S-1); S:=S-1
```

Similarly there are three statements (LG, LLG and SG) that provide access to global variables and three (LL, LLL and SL) that provide access to static ones.

Numerical constants may be loaded using LN which is defined as follows:

```
LN k   means  S:=S+1; P!(S-1):=k
```

The statement

```
LSTR k C1 C2 . . . Ck
```

will load onto the stack a value which represents the string composed of the characters whose integer codes are C1 to Ck.

The statements **TRUE** and **FALSE** load the corresponding truth values onto the stack.

Each expression operator replaces its operands, taken from the top of the stack, by its result. For instance, **MULT** is defined as follows:

```
MULT   means   P!(S-2):= P!(S-2)*P!(S-1); S:=S-1
```

Sixteen other dyadic expression operators are defined similarly. These are the integer operators **DIV**, **REM**, **PLUS** and **MINUS**, the relational operators **EQ**, **NE**, **LS**, **GR**, **LE** and **GE**, and the logical (or bit-pattern) operators **LSHIFT**, **RSHIFT**, **LOGAND**, **LOGOR**, **EQV** and **NEQV**.

There are three monadic expression operators defined as follows:

```
NEG   means   P!(S-1) := -P!(S-1)
NOT   means   P!(S-1) := NOT P!(S-1)
RV    means   P!(S-1) := !(P!(S-1))
```

Assignments to simple variables may already be translated using SP, SG and SL defined above; however, a statement is required for indirect assignments, defined as follows:

```
STIND   means   !(P!(S-1)) := P!(S-2); S:=S-2
```

Conditional commands in BCPL require corresponding conditional statements in OCODE. These are **JT Ln** and **JF Ln** which cause the program to jump conditionally to the label **Ln** depending on whether the top item of stack represents true or false. The label is set by the statement **LAB Ln** at the appropriate place in the program. Unconditional jumps are compiled into **JUMP** or **GOTO** which are defined as follows:

```
JUMP Ln   means   GOTO Ln
GOTO      means   S:=S-1; GOTO P!S
```

Occasionally it is necessary for the first phase of the compiler to tell the code generator where the top of the stack is, relative to P. This happens, for instance, when vectors are declared, or at the end of blocks. The OCODE statement to pass this information is **STACK k**, and its effect is to set S in the code generator to the value **k**. A second directive, STORE, is provided so that the first phase of the compiler can indicate the point dividing the declarations at the head of a block from the body that follows. Its effect is to cause the code generator to compile code to standardise the runtime state of the machine so that all stacked items are physically held in their appropriate store locations rather than being held in central processor registers. Without such a directive it would be difficult for an optimising code generator to know when stacked items could be held safely in machine registers.

The other OCODE statements relating to commands are SWITCHON, RES, RSTACK and FINISH, but these will not be described here.

The mechanism for procedure calls and the passing of parameters requires special care since there is such diversity in the instructions available on different machines for subroutine jumps. Efficient coding of these calls is particularly important since they occur frequently. For instance, in the BCPL compiler for the IBM 370 there are 1370 procedure calls in 23 000 words of compiled code. At the moment when control is about to be transferred to the called procedure, the runtime stack has the form shown in figure 7.3.

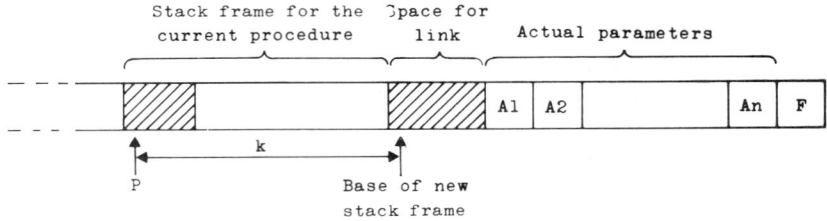

Fig. 7.3   The stack at the moment of call

The distance between the old and new stack frame pointers is a constant **k** which the compiler can determine for each call, being only dependent on the number of local variables and anonymous results that exist at the time. Since the parameters are always called by value, they can be evaluated and placed on the stack. Similarly the procedure entry point F is itself placed on the stack. The actual procedure call is made using FNAP **k** or RTAP **k** depending on whether the procedure should produce a result or not.

The entry point of the procedure is marked by the statement

ENTRY k Ln Cl C2 . . . Ck

where Ln is the symbolic label for the entry point and Cl to Ck are the characters of the name of the procedure. The ENTRY statement is immediately followed by a SAVE statement whose argument indicates the number of formal parameters the procedure has. The return from a procedure is caused by RTRN if there is no result, and by FNRN if there is a result to be returned.

These six statements allow the code generator writer considerable freedom in the design of the calling sequence for any particular machine. For instance, it is not difficult to generate code in which the first few arguments of a call are passed in central registers, which is a strategy well worth adopting for many reasons.

Static variables in BCPL are allocated storage cells at compile-time, using the ITEMN and ITEML statements. ITEMN k will allocate a static cell, giving it the initial value k where k is an integer, and ITEML Ln will allocate a static cell, giving it an initial value which represents the point in the program labelled Ln. Such static cells are themselves addressed by symbolic labels, which may be set by using the statement DATALAB Ln immediately preceding the corresponding ITEMN or ITEML statement.

The statement GLOBAL n globl labl ... globn labn causes the n global locations globl to globn to be initialised to values representing points in the program labelled labl to labn.

7.2.1 Example

As an example, the OCODE translation of the following program

```
GLOBAL $( START:1; WRITEF:76 $)
LET START() BE
$( LET F(N) = N = Ø -> 1, N*F(N-1)
   FOR I = 1 TO 1Ø DO WRITEF("F(%N) = %N*N", I, F(I))
$)
```

is

```
STACK 2
JUMP L2                             jump round the body of START
ENTRY 5 Ll 83 84 65 82 84  SAVE 2   entry to START
DATALAB L4 ITEML L3                 allocate cell for F
JUMP L5                             jump round the body of F
ENTRY 1 L3 70 SAVE 3                entry to F
LN Ø LP 2 EQ JF L7                  test if N=Ø
LN 1 JUMP L6                        then load 1 else
STACK 3
LAB L7 STACK 5
LP 2 LN 1 MINUS LL L4 FNAP 3        F(N-1)
LP 2 MULT                           multiplied by N
LAB L6
```

```
FNRN                                    return with result
STACK 2
LAB L5 STORE                            end of declarations
LN 1 STORE JUMP L8                      initialise the for-loop
LAB L9 STACK 5                          load arguments of WRITEF
LSTR 11 7Ø 4Ø 37 78 41                  load the string
       32 61 32 37 78 1Ø               "F(%N) = %N*N"
LP 2                                    load I
STACK 9 LP 2 LL L4 FNAP 7              call F(I)
LG 76 RTAP 3                            call WRITEF
LP 2 LN 1 PLUS SP 2                     increment I
LAB L8
LP 2 LN 1Ø LE JT L9                     loop again if I<=1Ø
STACK 2
RTRN                                    exit from START
STACK 2
LAB L2 STORE
GLOBAL 1
1 L1                                    initialise the global for START
```

7.3   *The code generator*

As has been seen, OCODE statements are simple and it is clear that code of
reasonable quality could not be generated by translating only one OCODE
statement at a time. Although it is impractical for the code generator to perform
global flow analysis, there are other areas of optimisation that are possible. It can,
for instance, perform local optimisation of register allocation and the selection of
machine instructions. Considerable benefit may be gained from a carefully chosen
global organisation. This includes the way that global and local variables are
accessed, together with the details of the calling sequence, particularly the way in
which registers are used to pass information to and from a called procedure. It is,
for instance, well worthwhile to place the first few arguments in central registers of
the machine if possible, and it is also a good idea to hold the result of a function call
in the same register that is used for the first argument. Even on machines with
many central registers it has been found to be a good strategy to re-use the
arguments registers to hold anonymous results during expression evaluation.

In order to perform the local optimisation, the code generator uses a simulated
model of the state of the computation in the target machine. This model varies in
complexity depending upon the level of optimisation desired. For many BCPL
code generators, the model consists solely of a simulation of the runtime stack in
which each item in the model represents an item held in the runtime stack. The
possible values that can be simulated by these items usually include constants,

simple variables and values held in central registers, and it is often possible to represent the addition of an integer constant and one level of indirection. This degree of simulation allows the code generator to produce respectable code, but still remain relatively simple. In fact many code generators share much of the program concerned with the input of OCODE and the simulation of the abstract machine, and so when embarking on a new BCPL implementation it is well worthwhile taking as a basis an already existing code generator for a similar machine.

We now describe some details of a typical code generator, with specific reference to one that was implemented for the XDS Sigma 7 (a 32-bit word-addressed multi-register machine). This code generator reads in each OCODE statement one at a time. If possible it just updates the simulated stack to represent the state of the computation after each statement, but if this is not possible it compiles some code in order to simplify the simulated model. Consider, for example, the translation of the BCPL statement

X := V!2

With suitable declarations of X and V the OCODE translation might be

```
LN  2       load the constant 2
LG  1ØØ     and load V
PLUS        add these values together
RV          indirect one level
SP  3       store the result in X
```

At the time when the code generator reads the PLUS statement, the top two items of the simulated stack hold elements representing the constant 2 and the hundredth global variable. The result of the PLUS operation can be accommodated in the model since the addition of a constant is provided for. Since indirection is also available, an item representing the entire expression V!2 is on top of the simulated stack at the time the SP statement is encountered.

Up to this point, no output has been produced. However, the SP statement necessitates the generation of some code. The code generator first checks whether optimisation is possible. For instance, if the top item of the simulated stack represents X+1 then it would be able to compile the BCPL statement into a single machine instruction. However, in this case it is not possible and the general assignment strategy is to compile a statement of the form

STW,r 3,P

where r is some general register holding the value of the right-hand side of the assignment, and 3,P is the machine-code address of X. Before this instruction can be compiled, a suitable value of r must be chosen and code compiled to move the top item of the stack into it. This code is generated by the function call MOVETOANYCR(ARG1), where ARG1 points to the item in the model representing the topmost element of the stack. This function inspects ARG1 to see if it represents one of the constants that are permanently held in central registers, but if this is not the case it calls the function MOVETOANYR(ARG1) to select a non-constant general register and to compile code to move ARG1 into it. If ARG1 represents a value that already involves a register, then that register is chosen, otherwise it selects a register that is free (as described below). Code to move ARG1 into this register is generated by the call MOVETOR(ARG1, r) which inspects ARG1 for optimisable special cases while also providing an adequate translation for all other cases.

By the algorithm just described, the code compiled for the statement X := V!2 on the Sigma 7 is as follows:

```
LW,R4    1ØØ,G    load V into R4
LW,R4    2,R4     load V!2 into R4
STW,R4   3,P      store it in X
```

When a general register is required, as it was in MOVETOANYR, the allocation is performed by a function called NEXTR. The strategy is to test the registers in fixed sequence and to select the first one that is free. This test involves searching all the items in the simulated stack but, since this is usually small, the cost is not great. If no register is available, then one is obtained by compiling code to dump a simulated stack item into store. The item that is chosen is as far as possible from the free end of the stack. This is a reasonable algorithm for register allocation and it has the merit that it does not tamper with the top two items of the stack which is important if we wish to keep the logic of the code generator simple.

Some BCPL code generators implement a simulation of the central registers in addition to the simulated stack. This allows optimisation of register use between statements such as one might expect in the compilation of

```
A := B
C := B
```

For example, on the IBM 370 implementation of BCPL this simulation is fairly complete and requires several pages of code for its implementation. However, effective optimisation of this sort is possible even with an extremely simple model. Again the Sigma 7 implementation is used as an example. The contents of only one register is simulated at any time using the variables SLAVEREG, SLAVEK and SLAVEN. The only values that can be represented in this model are simple variables. SLAVEREG gives the number of the machine register that currently holds the value of the variable, SLAVEK indicates whether the variable is local, global or static and SLAVEN is used to specify the corresponding relative address or label number. Whenever code is compiled that moves a simple variable into a register, the slave is updated. If the slave is empty when an assignment to a simple variable is made, the slave is updated appropriately and whenever code is compiled that invalidates the contents of the slave its contents are cleared. This may, for instance, be necessary after the compilation of an arithmetic instruction or an assignment to a simple variable. The slave must always be cleared on an indirect assignment since this can update any variable in store.

7.4   The bootstrapping process and INTCODE

In order to transfer BCPL to a new machine, it is necessary to write a new code generator for it. This can sometimes be written in BCPL and debugged on the donor machine. If this method is chosen it is usually best to generate assembly language which is then assembled and tested on the target machine. It is wise to defer most of the optimisation, since it complicates the code generator and increases the number of bugs, many of which will not be discovered until the compiled code is being tested on the target machine.

More often the installer has no access to the donor machine, and he must then resort to bootstrapping the compiler from a kit. The BCPL kit originally consisted of the source and OCODE forms of the compiler. However, the currently preferred approach is to use a different intermediate code specifically designed for the bootstrapping operation. This code is called INTCODE and is a compact and extremely simple assembly code. Typically it is possible to implement an INTCODE assembler and interpreter in less than one week.

Its purpose is to allow the installer to construct a temporary interpretive implementation on the target machine in the minimum time. This gives him the chance to learn the language and its compiler painlessly and allows him to write and debug the production code generator at his own installation. This method has been used many times and works well.

7.4.1   The INTCODE machine

The INTCODE machine has a store consisting of equal-sized locations addressed by consecutive integers. All INTCODE instructions have single and double length forms. The decision to use a double-length instruction depends partially upon the chosen field sizes, and is made by the INTCODE assembler. The central registers of the machine are as follows:

A, B: the accumulator and auxiliary accumulator,
C: the control register giving the location of the next instruction to be executed,

D: the address register, used to hold the effective address of an instruction,
P: a pointer used to address the current stack frame, and
G: a pointer used to address the global vector.

The format of an instruction comprises six fields as follows:

Function part: this is a three-bit field specifying one of the eight possible
                machine functions described below,
Address field: this is a field holding a positive integer which is the initial value
                of D,
D bit: a single bit which, when set, specifies that the initial value of D is to
                be taken from the following word,
P bit: a single bit to specify whether P is to be added into D at the second
                stage of address evaluation,
G bit: a single bit to specify whether G is to be added into D at the third
                stage of address evaluation, and
I bit: this is the indirection bit: if it is set then D is replaced by the
                contents of the location addressed by D at the last stage of address
                evaluation.

The effective address is evaluated the same way for every instruction independent of the particular machine function specified.

The eight machine functions are given by table 7.1.

Table 7.1   The INTCODE machine functions

Mnemonic	Operation	Specification
L	Load	`B := A; A := D`
S	Store	`!D := A`
A	Add	`A := A + D`
J	Jump	`C := D`
T	Jump if true	`IF A    THEN C := D`
F	Jump if false	`UNLESS A DO C := D`
K	Procedure call	`D := P + D`
		`D!Ø, D!1 := P, C`
		`P, C := D, A`
X	Execute operation	(miscellaneous operations, mainly arithmetical or logical operating on A and B – see program text, page 140 for details)

7.4.2   INTCODE assembly language

The assembly language for INTCODE has been designed to be compact and simple to assemble, but care has also been taken so that it can be read and modified with reasonable ease by a programmer. The text of the assembly language is composed of letters, digits, spaces, newlines, and the characters slash (/) and dollar ($). Slash is used as a continuation symbol; it is skipped and the remaining characters of the line up to and including the next newline character are ignored. Its main purpose is to simplify the efficient use of cards as a medium for transferring INTCODE programs. Dollar marks the entry point of a procedure, with the sole purpose of helping the implementer to find his way around the compiled code.

The assembly form of an instruction consists of the mnemonic letter for the machine function, optionally followed by I if indirection is specified, optionally followed by P or G if P or G modifications are specified, followed by the address which is either a signed integer or an assembly parameter of the form Ln, where n is an integer. Assembly parameters are used to label points in the program. A number not preceded by a letter is interpreted as a label and causes the specified assembly parameter to be set to the address of the next location to be loaded.

The statement Dk will allocate a static storage location initialised to the signed integer k. The statement DLn will allocate a static storage location initialised with the value of the assembly parameter Ln. Characters may be packed and assembled by using character statements of the form Ck where k is the integer code of the character. The character size and number of characters per word are machine dependent and it is left to the assembler to pack character strings and pad them appropriately with zeros.

It is possible to initialise global variables during assembly using a directive of the form GgLn. For example, G36L73 will cause global 36 of the INTCODE machine to be set to the value of assembly parameter number 73.

Z is used to mark the end of each segment of code. Its effect is to unset all the assembly parameters.

7.4.3 Example

As an example, the following program (which was also used in the discussion of OCODE)

```
GLOBAL $( START:1; WRITEF:76 $)
LET START( ) BE
$( LET F(N) = N=Ø -> 1, N*F(N-1)
   FOR I = 1 TO 1Ø DO WRITEF("F(%N) = %N*N", I, F(I))
$)
```

compiles into the following INTCODE:

```
$ 1 JL5
$ 3 LØ LIP2 X1Ø FL7 L1 SP3 JL6 7 LIP2 L1 X9 SP5 LIL4 K3 LIP2
X5 SP3 6 LIP3 X4
5 L1 SP2 JL8 9 LL499 SP5 LIP2 SP6 LIP2 SP9 LIL4 K7
SP7 LIG76 K3 LIP2 A1 SP2
8 LIP2 L1Ø X15 TL9 X4 2
4 DL3 499 C11 C7Ø C4Ø C37 C78 C41 C32 C61 C32 C37 C78 C1Ø
G1L1
Z
```

The effectiveness of INTCODE lies mainly in its simplicity making it easy to understand and implement; however, it is also compact and even with a simple non-optimising code generator the compiled code is smaller than straightforward machine code for most machines by a factor of nearly two to one. A typical INTCODE interpreter runs about ten times slower than compiled code on the same machine.

7.4.4 The INTCODE assembler and interpreter

To complete the description of INTCODE, we present the entire source of an INTCODE assembler and interpreter written in BCPL. This program assumes that string and character constants appearing in the INTCODE text use the ASCII code, but that it is to run on a 16-bit EBCDIC machine, hence the need for the ASCII and EBCDIC tables near the end. It has been tested on the IBM 370 (a 32-bit EBCDIC machine).

```
GET "LIBHDR"

MANIFEST $(
FSHIFT=13
DBIT=#1ØØØØ: PBIT=#4ØØØ; GBIT=#2ØØØ; IBIT=#1ØØØ
ABITS=#777
WORDSIZE=16; BYTESIZE=8; LABMAX=5ØØ
LIG1=#ØØ3ØØ1
K2  =#14ØØØ2
X22 =#16ØØ26
$)

GLOBAL $(
SYSPRINT:1ØØ; SOURCE:1Ø1; ETOA:1Ø2; ATOE:1Ø3
G:11Ø; P:111; CH:112; CYCLECOUNT:113
LABV:12Ø; CP:121; A:122; B:123; C:124; D:125; W:126  $)
```

```
LET ASSEMBLE() BE
$(1   LET V = VEC LABMAX
      LET F = Ø
      LABV := V


CLEAR:FOR I = Ø TO LABMAX TO LABV!I := Ø
      CP := Ø


NEXT: RCH()
SW:   SWITCHON CH INTO

$(S   DEFAULT: IF CH=ENDSTREAMCH RETURN
               WRITEF("*NBAD CH %C AT P = %N*N", CH, P)
               GOTO NEXT

      CASE 'Ø':CASE '1':CASE '2':CASE '3':CASE '4':
      CASE '5':CASE '6':CASE '7':CASE '8':CASE '9':
               SETLAB(RDN())
               CP := Ø
               GOTO SW

      CASE '$':CASE '*S':CASE '*N': GOTO NEXT

      CASE 'L': F := Ø; ENDCASE
      CASE 'S': F := 1; ENDCASE
      CASE 'A': F := 2; ENDCASE
      CASE 'J': F := 3; ENDCASE
      CASE 'T': F := 4; ENDCASE
      CASE 'F': F := 5; ENDCASE
      CASE 'K': F := 6; ENDCASE
      CASE 'X': F := 7; ENDCASE

      CASE 'C': RCH(); STC(RDN()); GOTO SW

      CASE 'D': RCH()
               TEST CH='L'
                 THEN $( RCH()
                         STW(Ø)
                         LABREF(RDN(), P-1)  $)
                 ELSE STW(RDN())
               GOTO SW
```

```
    CASE 'G': RCH()
              A := RDN() + G
              TEST CH='L' THEN RCH()
                  ELSE WRITEF("*NBAD CODE AT P = %N*N", P)
              !A := Ø
              LABREF(RDN(), A)
              GOTO SW

    CASE 'Z': FOR I = Ø TO LABMAX DO
                  IF LABV!I>Ø DO WRITEF("L%N UNSET*N", I)
              GOTO CLEAR  $)S


    W := F<<FSHIFT
    RCH()
    IF CH='I' DO $( W := W+IBIT; RCH() $)
    IF CH='P' DO $( W := W+PBIT; RCH() $)
    IF CH='G' DO $( W := W+GBIT; RCH() $)

    TEST CH='L'

      THEN $( RCH()
              STW(W+DBIT)
              STW(Ø)
              LABREF(RDN(), P-1)  $)

      ELSE $( LET A = RDN()
              TEST (A&ABITS)=A
                THEN STW(W+A)
                ELSE $( STW(W=DBIT); STW(A)  $)  $)

    GOTO SW   $)1

AND STW(W) BE $( !P := W
                 P, CP := P+1, Ø  $)

AND STC(C) BE $( IF CP=Ø DO $( STW(Ø); CP := WORDSIZE  $)
                 CP := CP - BYTESIZE
                 !(P-1) := !(P-1) + (C<<CP)  $)

AND RCH() BE $(1 CH := RDCH()
                UNLESS CH='/' RETURN
                UNTIL CH='*N' DO CH := RDCH()  $)1 REPEAT
```

```
AND RDN() = VALOF
    $( LET A, B = Ø, FALSE
       IF CH='-' DO $( B := TRUE; RCH() $)
       WHILE 'Ø'<=CH<='9' DO $( A := 1Ø*A+CH-'Ø'; RCH() $)
       IF B DO A := -A
       RESULTIS A $)


AND SETLAB(N) BE IF INRANGE(N) THEN
    $( LET K = LABV!N
       IF K<Ø THEN
         WRITEF("L%N ALREADY SET TO %N AT P = %N*N",N,-K,P)
       WHILE K>Ø DO $( LET N = !K
                        !K := P
                        K := N $)
       LABV!N := -P $)


AND LABREF(N, A) BE IF INRANGE(N) THEN
    $( LET K = LABV!N
       TEST K<Ø THEN K := -K OR LABV!N := A
       !A := !A + K $)


AND INRANGE(N) = VALOF
    $( IF Ø<=N<=LABMAX RESULTIS TRUE
       WRITEF("LABEL L%N OUT OF RANGE AT P = %N*N", N, P)
       RESULTIS FALSE $)


AND INTERPRET() = VALOF
$(1    CYCLECOUNT := CYCLECOUNT + 1
       W := !C
       C := C + 1

       TEST (W&DBIT)=Ø
         THEN D := W&ABITS
         ELSE $( D := !C; C := C+1 $)

       IF (W & PBIT) NE Ø THEN D := D + P
       IF (W & GBIT) NE Ø THEN D := D + G
       IF (W & IBIT) NE Ø THEN D := !D

       SWITCHON W>>FSHIFT INTO
```

```
$(  ERROR:
    DEFAULT: SELECTOUTPUT(SYSPRINT)
             WRITEF("*NINTCODE ERROR AT C = %N*N", C-1)
             RESULTIS -1

    CASE Ø: B := A; A := D;        LOOP
    CASE 1: !D := A;               LOOP
    CASE 2: A := A + D;            LOOP
    CASE 3: C := D;                LOOP
    CASE 4: IF A THEN C := D;      LOOP
    CASE 5: UNLESS A DO C := D;    LOOP
    CASE 6: D := P + D
            D!Ø, D!1 := P, C
            P, C := D, A
            LOOP


    CASE 7: SWITCHON D INTO

    $(  DEFAULT: GOTO ERROR

            CASE 1:  A := !A;          LOOP
            CASE 2:  A := -A;          LOOP
            CASE 3:  A := NOT A;       LOOP
            CASE 4:  C := P!1
                     P := P!Ø
                     LOOP
            CASE 5:  A := B * A;       LOOP
            CASE 6:  A := B / A;       LOOP
            CASE 7:  A := B REM A;     LOOP
            CASE 8:  A := B + A;       LOOP
            CASE 9:  A := B - A;       LOOP
            CASE 1Ø: A := B = A;       LOOP
            CASE 11: A := B NE A;      LOOP
            CASE 12: A := B < A;       LOOP
            CASE 13: A := B >= A;      LOOP
            CASE 14: A := B > A;       LOOP
            CASE 15: A := B <= A;      LOOP
            CASE 16: A := B << A;      LOOP
            CASE 17: A := B >> A;      LOOP
            CASE 18: A := B & A;       LOOP
            CASE 19: A := B | A;       LOOP
            CASE 2Ø: A := B NEQV A;    LOOP
            CASE 21: A := B EQV A;     LOOP
```

```
        CASE 22: RESULTIS Ø   // FINISH

        CASE 23: B, D := C!Ø, C!1   // SWITCHON
                 UNTIL B=Ø DO
                    $( B, C := B-1, C+2
                       IF A=C!Ø DO
                             $( D := C!1
                                BREAK $)  $)
                 C := D
                 LOOP


// cases 24 upwards are only called from the following
// hand-written INTCODE LIBRARY - ICLIB:

//    11 LIP2 X24 X4 G11L11 /SELECTINPUT
//    12 LIP2 X25 X4 G12L12 /SELECTOUTPUT
//    13 X26 X4       G13L13 /RDCH
//    14 LIP2 X27 X4 G14L14 /WRCH
//    42 LIP2 X28 X4 G42L42 /FINDINPUT
//    41 LIP2 X29 X4 G41L41 /FINDOUTPUT
//    30 LIP2 X30 X4 G30L30 /STOP
//    31 X31 X4 G31L31 /LEVEL
//    32 LIP3 LIP2 X32 G32L32 /LONGJUMP
//    46 X33 X4 G46L46 /ENDREAD
//    47 X34 X4 G47L47 /ENDWRITE
//    40 LIP3 LIP2 X35 G40L40 /APTOVEC
//    85 LIP3 LIP2 X36 X4 G85L85 / GETBYTE
//    86 LIP3 LIP2 X37 X4 G86L86 / PUTBYTE
//    Z

        CASE 24: SELECTINPUT(A); LOOP
        CASE 25: SELECTOUTPUT(A); LOOP
        CASE 26: A := ETOA!RDCH(); LOOP
        CASE 27: WRCH(ATOE!A); LOOP
        CASE 28: A := FINDINPUT(STRING37Ø(A)); LOOP
        CASE 29: A := FINDOUTPUT(STRING37Ø(A)); LOOP
        CASE 30: RESULTIS A  // STOP(A)
        CASE 31: A := P!Ø; LOOP  // used in LEVEL()
        CASE 32: P, C := A, B  // used in LONGJUMP(P,L)
                 LOOP
        CASE 33: ENDREAD(); LOOP
        CASE 34: ENDWRITE(); LOOP
```

```
           CASE 35: D := P+B+1    // used in APTOVEC(F, N)
                    D!Ø, D!1, D!2, D!3 := P!0, P!1, P, B
                    P, C := D, A
                    LOOP
           CASE 36: A := ICGETBYTE(A, B)  // GETBYTE(S, I)
                    LOOP
           CASE 37: ICPUTBYTE(A, B, P!4)  // PUTBYTE(S, I, CH)
                    LOOP
     $)  $)  $)1 REPEAT


AND STRING370(S) = VALOF
    $( LET T = TABLE Ø,Ø,Ø,Ø,Ø,Ø,Ø,Ø

       PUTBYTE(T, Ø, ICGETBYTE(S, Ø))
       FOR I = 1 TO ICGETBYTE(S,Ø) DO
              PUTBYTE(T,I,ATOE!ICGETBYTE(S,I))

       RESULTIS T  $)


AND ICGETBYTE(S, I) = VALOF
    $( LET W = S!(I/2)
       IF (I&1)=Ø DO W := W>>8
       RESULTIS W&255  $)


AND ICPUTBYTE(S, I, CH) BE
    $( LET P = ∂S!(I/2)
       LET W = !P
       TEST (I&1)=Ø THEN !P := W&#XØØFF | CH<<8
                    ELSE !P := W&#XFFØØ | CH      $)


LET START(PARM) BE
$(1

LET PROGVEC = VEC 2ØØØØ
LET GLOBVEC = VEC 4ØØ

G, P := GLOBVEC, PROGVEC

SYSPRINT := FINDOUTPUT("SYSPRINT")
SELECTOUTPUT(SYSPRINT)

WRITES("INTCODE SYSTEM ENTERED*N")
```

```
SOURCE := FINDINPUT("INTIN")
SELECTINPUT(SOURCE)
ASSEMBLE()
SOURCE := FINDINPUT("SYSIN")
UNLESS SOURCE=Ø DO SELECTINPUT(SOURCE)


WRITEF("*NPROGRAM SIZE = %N*N", P-PROGVEC)


ATOE := 1+TABLE -1,   // assuming ENDSTREAMCH=-1
     Ø,   Ø,   Ø,   Ø,   Ø,   Ø,   Ø,   Ø,  // ASCII to EBCDIC
     Ø,   5,  21,   Ø,  12,   Ø,   Ø,   Ø,  // '*T' '*N' '*P'
     Ø,   Ø,   Ø,   Ø,   Ø,   Ø,   Ø,   Ø,
     Ø,   Ø,   Ø,   Ø,   Ø,   Ø,   Ø,   Ø,


    64, 90,127,123, 91,108, 80,125, // '*S' ! " # $ % & '
    77, 93, 92, 78,107, 96, 75, 97, // ( ) * + , - . /
   240,241,242,243,244,245,246,247, // Ø 1 2 3 4 5 6 7
   248,249,122, 94, 76,126,110,111, // 8 9 : ; < = > ?
   124,193,194,195,196,197,198,199, // @ A B C D E F G
   200,201,209,210,211,212,213,214, // H I J K L M N O
   215,216,217,226,227,228,229,230, // P Q R S T U V W
   231,232,233, 66, 98, 67,101,102, // X Y Z [ \ ] ↑ ←
    64,129,130,131,132,133,134,135, // a b c d e f g
   136,137,145,146,147,148,149,150, // h i j k l m n o
   151,152,153,162,163,164,165,166, // p q r s t u v w
   167,168,169, 64, 79, 64, 95,255  // x y x | ¬


ETOA := 1+TABLE -1,   // assuming ENDSTREAMCH=-1
     Ø,   Ø,   Ø,   Ø,   Ø, #11,   Ø,   Ø,
     Ø,   Ø,   Ø, #13, #14, #15,   Ø,   Ø,
     Ø,   Ø,   Ø,   Ø,   Ø, #12,   Ø,   Ø,
     Ø,   Ø,   Ø,   Ø,   Ø,   Ø,   Ø,   Ø,
     Ø,   Ø,   Ø,   Ø,   Ø, #12,   Ø,   Ø,
     Ø,   Ø,   Ø,   Ø,   Ø,   Ø,   Ø,   Ø,
     Ø,   Ø,   Ø,   Ø,   Ø,   Ø,   Ø,   Ø,
     Ø,   Ø,   Ø,   Ø,   Ø,   Ø,   Ø,   Ø,
   #40,   Ø,#133,#135,   Ø,   Ø,   Ø,   Ø,
     Ø,   Ø,   Ø, #56, #74, #50, #53,#174,
   #46,   Ø,   Ø,   Ø,   Ø,   Ø,   Ø,   Ø,
     Ø,   Ø, #41, #44, #52, #51, #73,#176,
```

```
#55, #57, #134,    Ø,    Ø, #136, #137,    Ø,
  Ø,   Ø,   Ø, #54, #45, #14Ø,  #76,  #77,
  Ø,   Ø,   Ø,   Ø,   Ø,   Ø,    Ø,    Ø,
  Ø,   Ø, #72, #43, #1ØØ, #47,  #75,  #42,
  Ø, #141, #142, #143, #144, #145, #146, #147,
#15Ø, #151,   Ø,   Ø,   Ø,   Ø,    Ø,    Ø,
  Ø, #152, #153, #154, #155, #156, #157, #16Ø,
#161, #162,   Ø,   Ø,   Ø,   Ø,    Ø,    Ø,
  Ø,   Ø, #163, #164, #165, #166, #167, #17Ø,
#171, #172,   Ø,   Ø,   Ø,   Ø,    Ø,    Ø,
  Ø,   Ø,   Ø,   Ø,   Ø,   Ø,    Ø,    Ø,
  Ø,   Ø,   Ø,   Ø,   Ø,   Ø,    Ø,    Ø,
  Ø, #1Ø1, #1Ø2, #1Ø3, #1Ø4, #1Ø5, #1Ø6, #1Ø7,
#11Ø, #111,   Ø,   Ø,   Ø,   Ø,    Ø,    Ø,
  Ø, #112, #113, #114, #115, #116, #117, #12Ø,
#121, #122,   Ø,   Ø,   Ø,   Ø,    Ø,    Ø,
  Ø,   Ø, #123, #124, #125, #126, #127, #13Ø,
#131, #132,   Ø,   Ø,   Ø,   Ø,    Ø,    Ø,
 #6Ø,  #61,  #62,  #63,  #64,  #65,  #66,  #67,
 #7Ø,  #71,   Ø,   Ø,   Ø,   Ø,    Ø,    Ø


C := TABLE LIG1, K2, X22

CYCLECOUNT := Ø
A := INTERPRET()

SELECTOUTPUT(SYSPRINT)
WRITEF("*N*NEXECUTION CYCLES = %N, CODE = %N*N",
       CYCLECOUNT, A)
IF A<Ø DO MAPSTORE()
FINISH  $)1
```

8

Language definition

8.1   Program

At the outermost level, a BCPL program is a sequence of declarations.

8.2   Elements

```
<element> ::= <identifier> | <number> |
              <string constant> | <character constant> |
              TRUE | FALSE
```

An <identifier> consists of a sequence of letters, digits and dots, the first character of which must be a letter.

A <number> is either an integer consisting of a sequence of decimal digits, or an octal constant consisting of the character # followed by octal digits, or a hexadecimal constant consisting of #X followed by hexadecimal digits. The reserved words TRUE and FALSE are used to represent the two truth values.

A <string constant> consists of up to 255 characters enclosed in string quotes ("). Within a string, the character " may be represented only by the pair *" and the character * can only be represented by the pair **.

Other characters may be represented as follows:

        *N   is newline
        *T   is horizontal tab
        *S   is space
        *B   is backspace
        *P   is newpage

The internal representation of a string is the address of the region of store into which the length and characters of the string are packed.

A <character constant> consists of a single character enclosed in character quotes ('). The character ' can be represented in a character constant only by the pair *'. Other escape conventions are the same as for a string constant. A character constant is right justified in a word.

8.3   Expressions

All forms of expressions are listed below. E1, E2 and E3 represent arbitrary expressions except as noted in the descriptions which follow the list, and KØ, K1 and K2 represent constant expressions (whose values can be determined at compile-time, see section 8.3.8). C represents a command.

Primary	`<element>`	
	`( E1 )`	
Function call	`E1( )`	
	`E1( E2, E3, ...)`	
Addressing	`E1 ! E2`	subscripting
	`ə E1`	address generation
	`! E1`	indirection
Arithmetic	`E1 * E2`	
	`E1 / E2`	
	`E1 REM E2`	integer remainder
	`E1 + E2`	
	`+ E1`	
	`E1 - E2`	
	`- E1`	
Relational	`E1 = E2`	
	`E1 ¬= E2`	not equal
	`E1 < E2`	
	`E1 <= E2`	
	`E1 > E2`	
	`E1 >= E2`	
Shift	`E1 << E2`	left shift by E2 bits
	`E1 >> E2`	right shift by E2 bits
Logical	`¬ E1`	not (complement) E1
	`E1 & E2`	and
	`E1 | E2`	inclusive or
	`E1 EQV E2`	bitwise equivalence
	`E1 NEQV E2`	bitwise not-equivalence (exclusive or)
Conditional	`E1 -> E2, E3`	
Table	`TABLE KØ,K1,K2,...`	
Valof	`VALOF C`	see section 8.5.5.

The relative binding power of the operators is as follows:

(Highest, most binding)   Function call (see section 8.6.6)

                              `!` (subscripting)

                              `ə !`

                              `* / REM`

+ −
Relationals
Shifts (see section 8.3.4)
¬
&
|
EQV NEQV
−>
TABLE
(Lowest, least binding)   VALOF

In order that the rule allowing the omission of most semicolons should work properly, a dyadic operator may not be the first symbol on a line.

8.3.1   Addressing operators

If the value X is the address of a word in storage, then X+1 is the address of the next word.

If V is a variable, then associated with V is a single word of memory, which is called a cell. The contents of the cell is called the value of V and the address of the cell is called the address of V. An address may be used by applying the indirection operator (!). The expression

!E1

has, as value, the contents of the cell whose address is the value of the expression E1.

An address may be generated by means of the operator ∂. The expression

∂E1

is only valid if E1 is one of the following:

1. an identifier (not declared by a manifest declaration), in which case ∂V is the address of V,
2. a subscripted expression, in which case the value of ∂E1!E2 is E1+E2, or
3. an indirection expression, in which case the value of ∂!E1 is E1.

The interpretation of

!E1

depends on context as follows:

1. if it appears as the left hand side of an assignment statement

!E1:= E2

E1 is evaluated to produce the address of a cell and E2 is stored in it,

   2. ə(!E1) = E1 as noted above, or

   3. in any other context E1 is evaluated and the contents of that value, treated as an address, is taken.

Thus, ! forces one more contents-taking than is normally demanded by the context.

8.3.2 *Arithmetic operators*

The operators * and / denote integer multiplication and division. The operator **REM** yields the integer remainder after dividing the left-hand operand by the right hand one if both operands are positive, it is otherwise implementation dependent. The operators + and − may be used in either a monadic or dyadic context and perform the appropriate integer arithmetic operations. The treatment of arithmetic overflow is undefined.

8.3.3 *Relations*

A relational operator compares the integer values of its two operands and yields a truth-value (**TRUE** or **FALSE**) as result. The operators are as follows:

=	equal
¬=	not equal
<	less than
<=	less than or equal
>	greater than
>=	greater than or equal

   The operators = and ¬= make bitwise comparisons of their operands and so may be used to determine the equality of values regardless of the kind of objects they represent.

   An extended relational expression such as

'A'<=CH<='Z'

is equivalent to

'A'<=CH & CH<='Z'

8.3.4 Shift operators

In the expression E1<<E2 (or E1>>E2), E2 must evaluate to yield a non-negative integer. The value is E1, taken as a bit-pattern, shifted left (or right) by E2 places. Vacated positions are filled with zeroes.

Syntactically, the shift operators have lower precedence on the left than relational operators but greater precedence on the right. Thus, for example,

A >> 5 = 14   is equivalent to   (A>>5) = 14

whereas

14 = A >> 5   is equivalent to   (14=A) >> 5

8.3.5 Logical operators

The effect of a logical operator depends on context. There are two logical contexts: 'truth-value' and 'bit'. The truth-value context exists whenever the result of the expression will be interpreted immediately as true or false. In this case each sub-expression is interpreted, from left to right, in truth-value context until the truth or falsehood of the expression is determined. Then evaluation stops.

If an expression in a truth-value context yields neither true nor false the effect is undefined.

In a 'bit' context, the operator ¬ causes bit-by-bit complementation of its operand. The other operators combine their operands bit-by-bit according to the following table:

Operands		&	|	NEQV	EQV
0	0	0	0	0	1
0	1	0	1	1	0
1	0	0	1	1	0
1	1	1	1	0	1

8.3.6 The conditional operator

The expression

E1 -> E2, E3

is evaluated by evaluating E1 in truth-value context. If it yields true, then the expression has value E2, otherwise E3. E2 and E3 are never both evaluated.

8.3.7   Table

The value of the table expression

TABLE KØ, Kl, K2, ...

is the address of a static vector of cells initialised to the values of KØ, Kl, K2, ...
which must be constant-expressions.

8.3.8   Constant-expressions

A constant-expression is any expression involving only numbers, character
constants, names declared by manifest declarations, TRUE, FALSE and the opera-
tors *, /, REM, +, −, <<, >>, & and | .

8.4   Section brackets

Blocks, compound commands and some other syntactic constructions use the
symbols $(and $) which are called opening and closing section brackets. A
section bracket may be tagged with a sequence of letters, digits and dots (the same
characters as are used in identifiers).

   An opening section bracket can be matched only by an identically tagged closing
bracket. When the compiler finds a closing section bracket with a non-null tag, if
the nearest opening bracket (smallest currently open section) does not match, that
section is closed and the process repeats until a matching opening section bracket
is found. Thus is it impossible to write sections which are overlapping (not nested).

8.5   Commands

All forms of commands are listed below. E, El, E2, E3, Fl, F2 denote expressions,
K a constant-expression, C, Cl and C2 commands, and Dl and D2 declarations.

Routine call	E(El, E2, ...)
	E( )
Assignment	El, E2, ... := Fl, F2, ...
Conditional	IF E THEN C
	UNLESS E DO C
	TEST E THEN Cl ELSE C2

Repetitive	`WHILE E DO C`
	`UNTIL E DO C`
	`C REPEAT`
	`C REPEATWHILE E`
	`C REPEATUNTIL E`
	`FOR N = E1 TO E2 BY K DO C`
	`FOR N = E1 TO E2 DO C`
Resultis	`RESULTIS E`
Switchon	`SWITCHON E INTO` <compound command>
Transfer	`GOTO E`
	`FINISH`
	`RETURN`
	`BREAK`
	`LOOP`
	`ENDCASE`
Compound	`$( C1; C2; ... $)`
Block	`$( D1; D2; ...; C1; C2; ... $)`

Discussion of the routine call is deferred until section 8.6.6 where function and routine declarations are described.

8.5.1   *Assignment*

The command

`E1 : = F1`

causes the value of `F1` to be stored in the cell specified by `E1`. `E1` must have one of the following forms:

(1) the identifier of a variable   <identifier>
(2) a subscripted expression   `E2 ! E3`
(3) an indirection expression   `! E2`

In case (1), the cell belonging to the identifier is updated. Cases (2) and (3) have been described in section 8.3.1.

A list of assignments may be written thus:

`E1, E2, ..., En := F1, F2, ..., Fn`

where `Ei` and `Fi` are expressions. This is equivalent to

```
E1 := F1
E2 := F2
   ...
En := Fn
```

8.5.2   Conditional commands

```
IF E THEN C1
UNLESS E DO C2
TEST E THEN C1 ELSE C2
```

Expression `E` is evaluated in truth-value context. Command `C1` is executed if `E` is true, otherwise the command `C2` is executed.

8.5.3   The for-command

```
FOR N = E1 TO E2 BY K DO C
FOR N = E1 TO E2 DO C
```

`N` must be an identifier and `K` must be a constant expression. This command will be described by showing an equivalent block.

```
$( LET N, T = E1, E2
   UNTIL N>T DO $( C
                    N := N + K  $)
$)
```

If the value of `K` is negative the relation `N>T` is replaced by `N<T`. The declaration

```
LET N, T = E1, E2
```

declares two new cells with identifiers `N` and `T`, `T` being a new identifier that does not occur in `C`. Note that the control variable `N` is not available outside the scope of the command.

The command

```
FOR N = E1 TO E2 DO C
```

is equivalent to

```
FOR N = E1 TO E2 BY 1 DO C
```

8.5.4   Other repetitive commands

```
WHILE E DO C
UNTIL E DO C
C REPEAT
C REPEATWHILE E
C REPEATUNTIL E
```

Command C is executed repeatedly until condition E becomes true or false as implied by the command. If the condition precedes the command (WHILE, UNTIL) the test will be made before each execution of C. If it follows the command (REPEATWHILE, REPEATUNTIL), the test will be made after each execution of C. In the case of

```
C REPEAT
```

there is no condition and termination must be by a transfer or resultis-command in C. C will usually be a compound command or block.

Within REPEAT, REPEATWHILE and REPEATUNTIL, C is taken as short as possible. Thus, for example

```
IF E THEN C REPEAT
```

is the same as

```
IF E THEN $( C REPEAT $)
```

and

```
E := VALOF C REPEAT
```

is the same as

```
E := VALOF $( C REPEAT $)
```

8.5.5   Resultis-command and valof-expression

The expression

```
VALOF C
```

where C is a command (usually a compound command or block) is evaluated by executing the declarations and commands in C until a command of the form:

```
RESULTIS E
```

is encountered. The expression E is evaluated, its value becomes the value of the valof-expression (which must be in the current procedure body) and execution of the commands within C ceases. A valof-expression must contain one or more resultis-commands and one must be executed. In the case of nested valof-expressions, the resultis-command terminates only the innermost valof-expression containing it.

8.5.6   Switchon-command

```
SWITCHON E INTO <compound command>
```

where the compound command contains labels of the form

```
CASE K:
```

or

```
DEFAULT:
```

The expression E is first evaluated and, if a case exists which has a constant with the same value, then execution is resumed at that label; otherwise, if there is a default label, then execution is continued from there, and if there is not then execution is resumed from just after the end of the switchon-command.

8.5.7   Transfer of control

```
GOTO E
FINISH
RETURN
BREAK
LOOP
ENDCASE
```

The command GOTO E interprets the value of E as the address of a point in the program (which must be in the current procedure body), and transfers control to that point. The command FINISH causes an implementation-dependent termination of the entire program. RETURN causes control to return to the caller of a routine. BREAK causes execution to be resumed at the point just after the smallest textually enclosing repetitive command. The repetitive commands are those with the following key words:

UNTIL, WHILE, REPEAT, REPEATWHILE, REPEATUNTIL, FOR.

LOOP causes execution to be resumed at the point just before the end of the body of a repetitive command. For a for-command it is the point where the control variable is incremented, and for the other repetitive commands it is where the condition (if any) is tested. ENDCASE causes execution to be resumed at the point just after the smallest textually enclosing switchon-command.

8.5.8   *Compound command*

A compound command is a sequence of commands enclosed in section brackets.

$(C1; C2; ... $)

the commands C1, C2, ... are executed in sequence.

8.5.9   *Block*

A block is a sequence of declarations followed by a sequence of commands enclosed together in section brackets.

$(D1; D2; ... ; C1; C2; ... $)

The declarations D1, D2, ... and the commands C1, C2, ... are executed in sequence. The scope of an identifier (i.e. the region of program where the identifier is known) declared in a declaration is the declaration itself (to allow recursive definition), the subsequent declarations and the commands of the block. Notice that the scope does not include earlier declarations or extend outside the block.

8.6   *Declarations*

Every identifier used in a program must be declared explicitly. All forms of declaration are shown below, where N, N1, N2 are names, K, K1, K2 are constant expressions, and E, E1, E2 are expressions.

Global	`GLOBAL $( N1:K1; N2:K2; ... $)`
Manifest	`MANIFEST $( N1=K1; N2=K2; ... $)`
Static	`STATIC $( N1=K1; N2=K2; ... $)`
Dynamic	`LET N1, N2, ... = E1, E2, ...`
Vector	`LET N = VEC K`
Function	`LET N(N1, N2, ... ) = E`
Routine	`LET N(N1, N2, ... ) BE C`
Formal parameter	(these occur as part of function and routine declarations)
Label	`N:`
For-loop	`FOR N = E1 TO E2 BY K TO C`

The declaration of formal parameters is covered in sections 8.6.6 and 8.6.7, and the for-loop is described in section 8.5.3. The scope of identifiers declared at the head of a block is described in the previous section.

8.6.1 Global

A BCPL program need not be compiled in one piece. The sole means of communication between separately compiled segments of program is the global vector. The declaration

```
GLOBAL $( N1:K1 $)
```

associates the identifier N1 with the location K1 in the global vector. This name identifies a static cell which may be accessed by name or by any other identifier associated with the same global vector location.

   Global declarations may be combined. The declaration

```
GLOBAL $( N1:K1; N2:K2; ...; Nn:Kn $)
```

is equivalent to

```
GLOBAL  $( N1:K1  $)
GLOBAL  $( N2:K2  $)
...
GLOBAL  $( Nn:Kn  $)
```

8.6.2   Manifest

An identifier may be associated with a constant by the declaration

```
MANIFEST $( N1=K1 $)
```

An identifier declared by a manifest declaration may only be used in contexts where a constant would be allowable. It may not, for instance, appear on the left-hand side of an assignment. Like global declarations, manifest declarations may be combined. The declaration

```
MANIFEST $( N1=K1; N2=K2; ...; Nn=Kn $)
```

is equivalent to

```
MANIFEST  $(  N1=K1  $)
MANIFEST  $(  N2=K2  $)
...
MANIFEST  $(  Nn=Kn  $)
```

8.6.3   Static

A variable may be declared and given an initial value by the declaration

```
STATIC $( N1=K1 $)
```

The variable N1 has a cell permanently allocated to it throughout the execution of the program (even when control is not dynamically within the scope of the declaration). Like global declarations, static declarations may be combined. The declaration

```
STATIC $( N1=K1; N2=K2; ...; Nn=Kn $)
```

is equivalent to

```
STATIC  $(  N1=K1  $)
STATIC  $(  N2=K2  $)
...
STATIC  $(  Nn=Kn  $)
```

8.6.4   *Dynamic*

The declaration

```
LET N1, N2, ..., Nn = E1, E2, ..., En
```

creates dynamic cells and associates with them the identifiers N1, N2, ..., Nn. These cells are initialised to the values of E1, E2, ..., En. The space reserved for these cells is released on leaving the block in which the declaration appears. The order of initialisation of N1...Nn is not defined.

8.6.5   *Vector*

The declaration

```
LET N = VEC K
```

where K is a constant-expression, creates a dynamic vector by reserving K+1 cells of contiguous storage in memory, plus one cell which is associated with the identifier N. Execution of the declaration causes the value of N to become the address of the K+1 cells. The storage allocated is released on leaving the block.

8.6.6   *Procedure*

The declaration

```
LET N(N1, N2, ..., Nm) = E
```

declares a function named N with m parameters. The parentheses are required even if m = 0. A parameter name has the same syntax as an identifier, and its scope is the expression E. A routine declaration is similar to a function declaration except that its body is a command:

```
LET N(N1, N2, ..., Nm) BE C
```

If the declaration is within the scope of a global declaration for N, then the global cell will be initialised to the entry address of the procedure before execution of the program. Otherwise, a static cell is created, associated with the identifier N and initialised to the entry address.

The procedure is invoked by the call

```
E( E1, E2, ... )
```

where expression **E** evaluates to the entry address. In particular, within the scope of the identifier **N**, the procedure may be invoked by the call

```
N( E1, E2, ... )
```

provided the value of **N** has not been changed during the execution of the program.

Each value passed as a parameter is copied into a newly created cell which is then associated with the corresponding parameter name. The cells are consecutive in store and so the argument list behaves like an initialised dynamic vector. The space allocated for the argument list is released when evaluation of the call is complete. The arguments are always passed by value; however, the value passed may, of course, be an address. The number of parameters passed in a call of a procedure need not equal the number of formal parameters in the procedure declaration. Implications of this are discussed in section 4.2.3. A function call is a call in the context of an expression. If a function is being called, the result is the value of **E**, and if a routine is being called, the result is undefined. A routine call is a call in the context of a command and may be used to call either a function or a routine. A routine call has no result. No dynamic (or vector or formal) variable that is declared outside a procedure may be directly referred to from within its body.

8.6.7 Label

A label may be declared by

```
N:
```

A label declaration may precede any command or label declaration, but may not precede any other form of declaration. Exactly as in the case of a procedure declaration, a label declaration creates a static cell if it is not within the scope of a global declaration of the same identifier. The static or global cell is initialised before execution with the address of the point in the program labelled, so that the command

```
GOTO N
```

has the expected effect.

The scope of a label depends on its context. It is the smallest of the following regions of program:

(1) the command sequence of the smallest textually enclosing block,
(2) the body of the smallest textually enclosing valof-expression or procedure,
(3) the body of the smallest textually enclosing for-command.

Using a goto-command to transfer to a label which is outside the current procedure will produce undefined results.

8.6.8 Simultaneous declaration

Any declaration of the form

`LET ...`

may be followed by one or more declarations of the form

`AND ...`

where any construct which may follow `LET` may follow `AND`. As far as scope is concerned, such a collection of declarations is treated like a single declaration. This makes it possible, for example, for two procedures to know each other without recourse to the global vector. The order of declaration of items connected by `AND` is not defined.

8.7 Miscellaneous features

8.7.1 Get-directives

It is possible to include a file in the source text of a program using a get-directive of the form:

`GET "string"`

where `string` is an implementation-dependent file specifier. A get-directive should appear on a line by itself.

8.7.2 Comments and spaces

The character pair // denotes the beginning of a comment. All characters from (and including) // up to but not including the newline character will be ignored by the compiler. Blank lines are also ignored. Space and tab characters may be inserted freely except inside an element, a reserved word (e.g. VALOF), or an operator (e.g. :=). Space or tab characters are required to separate identifiers or system words from adjoining identifiers or system words.

8.7.3   Optional symbols and synonyms

The reserved words DO and THEN are synonyms in BCPL, as are OR and ELSE. Most implementations of BCPL also allow other synonyms.

In order to make BCPL programs easier to read and to write, the compiler allows the syntax rules to be relaxed in certain cases. The word DO (or THEN) may be omitted whenever it is immediately followed by the keyword of a command (e.g. RESULTIS). Any semicolon occurring as the last symbol of a line may be omitted.

8.8   The formal syntax of BCPL

This section presents the Backus Naur form (BNF) of the syntax of BCPL. The whole syntax is given, with the following exceptions:

1. Comments are not included, and the space character is not represented even where required.
2. The section-bracket tagging rule is not included, since it is impossible to represent in BNF.
3. The graphic escape sequences allowable in string and character constants are not represented.
4. No account is made of the rules which allow dropping of semicolon and DO in most cases. These rules unnecessarily complicate the BNF syntax yet are easy to understand by other means.
5. BCPL has several synonymous system words and operators: for example, DO and THEN. Only a standard form of these symbols is shown in the syntax.
6. Certain constructions can be used only in specific contexts. Not all these restrictions are included: for example, CASE and DEFAULT can only be used in switches, and RESULTIS only in expressions. Finally, there is the necessity of declaring all identifiers that are used in a program.
7. There is a syntactic ambiguity relating to <repeated command> which is resolved in section 8.5.4

The brackets [ ] imply arbitrary repetition of the categories enclosed.

8.8.1   *Identifiers, strings, numbers*

<letter>	::=	A | B | C | D | E | F | G | H | I | J | K | L | M | N | O | P | Q | R | S | T | U | V | W | X | Y | Z
<octal digit>	::=	Ø | 1 | 2 | 3 | 4 | 5 | 6 | 7
<hex digit>	::=	Ø | 1 | 2 | 3 | 4 | 5 | 6 | 7 | 8 | 9 | A | B | C | D | E | F
<digit>	::=	Ø | 1 | 2 | 3 | 4 | 5 | 6 | 7 | 8 | 9
<string constant>	::=	"<255 or fewer characters>"
<character constant>	::=	' <one character> '
<octal number>	::=	# <octal digit> [<octal digit>]
<hex number>	::=	#X <hex digit> [<hex digit>]
<number>	::=	<octal number> | <hex number> | <digit> [<digit>]
<identifier>	::=	<letter> [<letter> | <digit> | .]

8.8.2   *Operators*

<address op>	::=	@ | !
<mult op>	::=	* | / | REM
<add op>	::=	+ | −
<rel op>	::=	= | ¬= | <= | >= | < | >
<shift op>	::=	<< | >>
<and op>	::=	&
<or op>	::=	|
<eqv op>	::=	EQV | NEQV
<not op>	::=	¬

8.8.3   *Expressions*

<element>	::=	<character constant> | <string constant> | <number> | <identifier> | TRUE | FALSE
<primary E>	::=	<primary E> (<expression list>) | <primary E> ( ) | (<expression>) | <element>
<vector E>	::=	<vector E> ! <primary E> | <primary E>
<address E>	::=	<address op> <address E> | <vector E>
<mult E>	::=	<mult E> <mult op> <address E> | <address E>
<add E>	::=	<add E> <add op> <mult E> | <add op> <mult E> | <mult E>
<rel E>	::=	<add E> [<rel op> <add E>]
<shift E>	::=	<shift E> <shift op> <add E> | <rel E>
<not E>	::=	<not op> <shift E> | <shift E>
<and E>	::=	<not E> [<and op> <not E>]

```
<or E>                    :: =   <and E> [ <or op> <and E> ]
<eqv E>                   :: =   <or E> [ <eqv op> <or E> ]
<conditional E>           :: =   <eqv E> -> <conditional E> , <conditional E> |
                                 <eqv E>
<expression>              :: =   <conditional E> |
                                 TABLE <constant expression>
                                                 [, <constant expression>] |
                                 VALOF <command>
```

8.8.4   Constant-expressions

```
<c element>               :: =   <character constant> | <number> | <identifier> |
                                 TRUE | FALSE | (<constant expression>)
<c mult E>                :: =   <c mult E> <mult op> <c element> | <c element>
<c add E>                 :: =   <c add E> <add op> <c mult E> |
                                 <add op> <c mult E> | <c mult E>
<c shift E>               :: =   <c shift E> <shift op> <c add E> | <c add E>
<c and E>                 :: =   <c and E> <and op> <c shift E> | <c shift E>
<constant expression>     :: =   <constant expression> <or op> <c and E> |
                                 <c and E>
```

8.8.5   Lists of expressions and identifiers

```
<expression list>         :: =   <expression> [ , <expression> ]
<name list>               :: =   <name> [ , <name> ]
```

8.8.6   Declarations

```
<manifest item>           :: =   <identifier> = <constant expression>
<manifest list>           :: =   <manifest item> [ ; <manifest item> ]
<manifest declaration>    :: =   MANIFEST $( <manifest list> $)
<static declaration>      :: =   STATIC $( <manifest list> $)
<global item>             :: =   <identifier> : <constant expression>
<global list>             :: =   <global item> [ ; <global item> ]
<global declaration>      :: =   GLOBAL $( <global list> $)
<simple definition>       :: =   <name list> = <expression list>
<vector definition>       :: =   <identifier> = VEC <constant expression>
<function definition>     :: =   <identifier> (<name list>) = <expression> |
                                 <identifier> ( ) = <expression>
<routine definition>      :: =   <identifier> (<name list>) BE <command> |
                                 <identifier> ( ) BE <command>
```

<definition>	::=	<simple definition> | <vector definition> | <function definition> | <routine definition>
<simultaneous declaration>	::=	LET <definition> [AND <definition>]
<declaration>	::=	<simultaneous declaration> | <manifest declaration> | <static declaration> | <global declaration>

8.8.7 Left-hand side expressions

| <lhse> | ::= | <identifier> \| <vector E> ! <primary E> \|
! <primary E> |
| <left hand side list> | ::= | <lhse> [, <lhse>] |

8.8.8 Unlabelled commands

<assignment>	::=	<left hand side list> := <expression list>
<simple command>	::=	BREAK | LOOP | ENDCASE | RETURN | FINISH
<goto command>	::=	GOTO <expression>
<routine command>	::=	<primary E> (<expression list>) | <primary E> ( )
<resultis command>	::=	RESULTIS <expression>
<switchon command>	::=	SWITCHON <expression> INTO <compound command>
<repeatable command>	::=	<assignment> | <simple command> | <goto command> | <routine command> | <resultis command> | <repeated command> | <switchon command> | <compound command> | <block>
<repeated command>	::=	<repeatable command> REPEAT | <repeatable command> REPEATUNTIL <expression> | <repeatable command> REPEATWHILE <expression>
<until command>	::=	UNTIL <expression> DO <command>
<while command>	::=	WHILE <expression> DO <command>
<for command>	::=	FOR <identifier> = <expression> TO <expression> BY <constant expression> DO <command> | FOR <identifier> = <expression> TO <expression> DO <command>
<repetitive command>	::=	<repeated command> | <until command> | <while command> | <for command>

\<test command\>	:: =	TEST \<expression\> THEN \<command\> ELSE \<command\>
\<if command\>	:: =	IF \<expression\> THEN \<command\>
\<unless command\>	:: =	UNLESS \<expression\> THEN \<command\>
\<unlabelled command\>	:: =	\<repeatable command\> | \<repetitive command\> | \<test command\> | \<if command\> |

8.8.9 Labelled commands

\<label prefix\>	:: =	\<identifier\> :
\<case prefix\>	:: =	CASE \<constant expression\> :
\<default prefix\>	:: =	DEFAULT :
\<prefix\>	:: =	\<label prefix\> | \<case prefix\> | \<default prefix\>
\<command\>	:: =	\<unlabelled command\> | \<prefix\> \<command\> | \<prefix\>

8.8.10 Blocks and compound commands

\<command list\>	:: =	\<command\> [; \<command\>]
\<declaration part\>	:: =	\<declaration\> [; \<declaration\>]
\<block\>	:: =	$(\<declaration part\> ; \<command list\> $)
\<compound command\>	:: =	$(\<command list\> $)
\<program\>	:: =	\<declaration part\>

References

[1]   Barron, D. W., Buxton, J. N., Hartley, D. F., Nixon, E. and Strachey, C. The main features of CPL. *Computer Journal*, vol. 6, p. 134 (1963)

[2]   Barron, D. W. *Recursive techniques in programming*. MacDonald/Elsevier Computer Monographs no. 3 (1968)

[3]   Birtwistle, G. M., Dahl, O. J., Myhrhaug, B. and Nygaard, K. *Simula Begin*. Auerbach Publications (1973)

[4]   Brown, P. J. (ed.) *Software portability*. Cambridge University Press (1977)

[5]   Canaday, R. H. and Richie, D. M. *The BCPL programming manual*. Bell Laboratories, Murray Hill, N.J. (1969)

[6]   Kernighan, B. W. *Programming in C – a tutorial*. Bell Laboratories, Murray Hill, N.J. (1972)

[7]   Liskov, B., Snyder, A., Atkinson, R. and Schaffert, C. Abstract mechanisms in CLU. *Communications of the Association for Computing Machinery*, vol. 20, no. 8, p. 564 (1977)

[8]   Morris, J. H. *The BCPL programming manual*. University of California, Berkeley (1970)

[9]   Parnas, D. L. On the criteria to be used on decomposing a system into modules. *Communications of the Association for Computing Machinery*, vol. 15, no. 12, p. 1053 (1972)

[10]   Richards, M. BCPL – a tool for compiler writing and systems programing. *Proceedings of the Spring Joint Computer Conference*, vol. 34, pp. 557–66 (1969)

[11]   Richards, M. The portability of the BCPL compiler. *Software, Practice and Experience*, vol. 1, no. 2 (1971)

[12]   Stoy, J. E. and Strachey, C. OS6 – an experimental operating system for a small computer. Part 2: Input/output and filing system. *Computer Journal*, vol. 15, no. 3, p. 195 (1972)

[13]   Stoy, J. E. and Strachey, C. *Text of OS6*. Oxford Programming Research Group Monographs

[14]   Stoy, J. E. and Strachey, C. *Commentary on OS6*. Oxford Programming Research Group Monographs

INDEX

SYMBOLS

!   20, 30, 147
%   58
#*   57
#+   57
#−   57
#/   57
#<   57
#<=   57
#=   57
#>   57
#>=   57
#¬=   57
$(8, 14, 150
$)   8, 14, 150
&   13, 39, 40
*   10, 17, 145, 146, 148
*'   9, 145
**   10, 145
*B   9, 145
*P   9, 145

*S   9, 145
*T   9, 145
+   17, 146, 148
−   17, 146, 148
/   17, 146, 148
//   9, 160
<   13, 146, 148
<<   40, 146, 149
<=   13, 146, 148
=   13, 146, 148
>   13, 146, 148
>=   13, 146, 148
>>   40, 146, 149
:   41, 159
:=   9, 151
ə   30, 36, 146, 147
¬   13, 40, 146, 147
¬=   13, 146, 148
| 13, 40, 146, 147

A

ABORT   63, 78
abstract object   1
actual parameter   21, 35, 159
address generation expressions   30, 146
addressing operators   30, 147
AE tree   79, 98
Algol 60   3, 7, 8, 74, 76, 77
analysis of commands   118
analysis of definitions   116
analysis of expressions   110
AND   22, 75, 160
applicative expression tree   79, 98
APTOVEC   54
arithmetic   17, 148
arithmetic expressions   9, 17, 146
arithmetic operators   17, 148
ASCII   9

assembler and interpreter for
     INTCODE   136
assignment command   9, 150, 151

B

BACKTRACE   63
binding of operators   40, 146
bit context   149
bit operations   39, 146, 149
bit-pattern   1, 2, 42
block   14, 151, 155
bootstrapping   133
brackets, use of   40
break-command (BREAK)   38, 154

C

C programming language   42
call-by-value   35, 76, 159
capital letters   3
CASE label   27, 154
cell   1
CG   79
CH   82
character constant   9, 145
character set   3
CHARCODE   88
CHECKFOR   108
code generator   79, 125, 130
code optimisation   130
colon   41, 159
colon, missing   60
commands   4, 150
commands, analysis of   118
comments   9, 160
compilation, separate   5, 45
compiler   5, 79, 124
compiler portability   124
compound commands   13, 14, 150, 152
conceptual types   2, 34
conditional commands   13, 17, 150, 152
conditional expression   17, 18, 146
conditional operator   18, 149
constant, character   9, 145
constant, decimal integer   9, 145
constant, hexadecimal   145
constant, octal   9, 145
constant, string   23, 145
constant-expression   16, 150
constants   9, 145
context determination of type   42
context, bit   149
context, truth-value   41, 149
controlled variable   16, 152
CPL   1
cross-compiler   5

D

dangling references   76
data types   2, 42
DEBUG   67
debugging   60
decimal integer constant   9, 145
declarations   3, 4, 8, 21, 22, 25, 26, 42,
      45, 155
declarations, simultaneous   22, 75, 160
DECLSYSWORDS   92
DECVAL   82
DEFAULT   27, 154
definitions, analysis of   116
division   17, 148

DO   17, 161
DO needed   61
DYADIC   114
dynamic free variable   26, 62
dynamic variable declaration   8, 158
dynamic variables   4, 8, 25, 62

E

EBCDIC   9
elements   145
end-of-line   9, 145
ENDCASE   27, 154
ENDCASE, omission of   76
ENDSTREAMCH   11, 47
EQV   40, 146, 147
error handling at runtime   62
error handling   60
errors, semantic   62
escape conventions   9, 145
expressions   4, 9, 16, 17, 18, 30, 146, 150
expressions, analysis of   110
extended relational expression   13, 148
extent   4
extra semicolons   60

F

FALSE   145
field-selector   57
FINDFILE   47
FINDINPUT   47
FINDOUTPUT   47
FINISH   154
FIX   57
FLOAT   57
floating point   57
for-command   16, 152
formal parameter   2, 35, 159
formal syntax of BCPL   161
formatted output   50
FORMTREE   100
Fortran   3, 7, 13, 76
free variables, dynamic,   26, 62
FREEBLK   55
freestore management   55
function call   7, 22, 159
function declaration   22, 158
functions   4, 7, 22

G

get-directive   8, 45, 160
GETBLK   55
GETBYTE   23, 49, 59

global declaration   26, 156
global variable   25, 74
global variables, misuse of   74
global vector   4, 26, 45, 156
GOTO, erroneous use of   76
goto-command (GOTO)   41, 154, 159

H

hexadecimal constant   145

I

I/O   11, 47
identifier (name)   8, 145
if-command (IF)   13, 152
IGNORE   108
indirection   1, 30, 147
indirection expressions   146
input and output   11, 47
input and output library   48
INTCODE   133
INTCODE assembler and
    interpreter   136
INTCODE assembly language   134
INTCODE example   135
INTCODE machine   133
integer representation   17
internal types   2
interpreter for INTCODE   136

L

label   41, 159
language definition   145
language extensions   47
LASSOC   114
LET ... AND   22, 79, 160
let-declaration (LET)   8
LEVEL   52
lexical analyser   79
library   5, 47
local variables   8, 25
logical expressions   39, 146
logical operators   39, 49
LOOKUPWORD   84, 90
loop-command (LOOP)   39, 154
lower-case letters   3

M

machine independence   47
manifest constant   2, 10, 157

manifest declaration   10, 157
MAPSTORE   63
matrices   33
MAXCOM   67
mismatched parameters   77
mismatched section brackets   61
missing colon   60
missing procedure   74
ModComp II   67
modularity   4
modulo (remainder) operator   17, 146,
    148
MULDIV   52
multiplication   17, 148

N

names (identifiers)   8, 145
name, multiple use of   75
NAMETABLE   90
NAMETABLESIZE   90
NEEDS   27
NEQV   40, 146, 149
newline, use of   7, 9, 160
NEWVEC   90, 100
NEXTSYMB   80, 82
NLPENDING   82
NULLTAG   94
number   9, 145

O

object machine   1, 124
OCODE   79, 125
OCODE example   129
octal constant   9, 145
operations   2
operator precedence   40, 146
operator precedence errors   77
operators   17, 18, 30, 39, 146, 147, 149
operators, omission of   76
optimisation of code   130
optional symbols   161
OS6 stream structure   43
output   11, 47
output, mis-selection of   78
overflow   17

P

PACKSTRING   24, 50
parameter (actual)   21, 35, 159

parameter (formal)   21, 35, 159
parameter passing   35, 159
parameter mismatch   77
PERFORMGET   84, 96
PL/I   7, 77
pointers   30
pointers, misuse of   75
portability   5
portability (compiler)   124
potholes and traps   73
precedence errors   77
precedence of operators   40, 146
precompilation   5
primary expressions   146
procedure call   21, 43, 159
procedure declaration   21, 42, 45, 158
procedure values   42, 158
procedure values, misuse of   74
procedure   4, 21, 42, 45, 158
procedure, missing   74
profile   67
program   145
PUTBYTE   3, 23, 49, 59

R

RANDOM   52
RBCOM   118
RBEXP   110
RCOM   122
RDBLOCKBODY   104
RDCDEFS   106
RDCH   11, 47
RDEF   116
RDSECT   108
RDSEQ   104
RDSTRCH   88
RDTAG   84, 94
READN   12, 48
READNUMBER   82, 96
REC.P, REC.L   102
recursion   36
relational expressions   13, 146
relational operators   13, 146, 148
relations   13, 148
relations, extended /   13, 148
remainder operator (REM)   17, 146, 148
REPEAT   16, 153
REPEATUNTIL   16, 153
REPEATWHILE   14, 153
repetitive commands   14, 151, 153
reserved words   3
resultis-command (RESULTIS)   22, 151,
      154

return-command (RETURN)   22, 154
REXP   82, 112
REXPLIST   117
RNAME   108
RNAMELIST   33, 108
routine call commands   7, 159
routine declaration   158
routines   4
runtime error handling   62
runtime errors   74
runtime stack   126

S

scope   4
scope of a label   160
scope rules   38, 155
section brackets   8, 14, 150
section brackets, mismatched   61
SELECTINPUT   11, 47
selectors (H1,...,H5)   90
SELECTOUTPUT   11, 47
semantic errors   62
semicolon   9, 161
semicolon, extra   60
semicolons, omissions of   147
separate compilation   5, 45, 74
shift expressions   40, 146
shift operators   40, 149
simultaneous declaration   22, 160
simultaneous declarations, misuse of   75
SLCT   58
space, use of   9, 160
stack mechanism   62
START   7
static declaration   44, 157
static variables   4, 44, 157
storage cell   1
store   1
store management   55
streams   11
string constant   145
string problems   62
string, internal representation   31, 49,
      145
strings   23, 49, 145
subscription expressions   146
subscripts, misuse of   75
switchon-command   27, 151, 154
SYMB   80
SYN   79
synonyms   161
SYNREPORT   102
syntax error   60
syntax of BCPL   3, 161

T

table (TABLE) 32, 150
table expressions 146
tabs 160
tagged section brackets 14, 161
tagging, inadvertant 61
target code 79, 125
TEST 17, 150, 152
THEN 17, 150, 152
THEN needed 61
TRACE 67
transfer commands 151
transfer of control 154
TREEVEC 100
TRN 79
TRUE 145
truth values 14
truth-value context 41, 149
type determination by context 42
types, conceptual 2, 34
types, internal 2

U

uninitialised variables 78
UNLESS 13, 17, 150, 152
UNPACKSTRING 24, 50
UNTIL 16, 151, 153

V

valof-expression (VALOF) 22, 146, 154
value 1, 2
variable declarations 8, 155
variable names 8
variables 2, 8, 25
variables, uninitialised 78
vector declaration 20, 31, 158
vector, global 4, 26, 45, 156
vectors as procedure parameters 36
vectors of characters 23

W

WHILE 14, 153
WORDNODE 82, 90
WORDSIZE 82, 90
WRCH 11, 47
WRITED 48
WRITEF 13, 50
WRITEHEX 49
WRITEN 8, 48
WRITEOCT 49
WRITES 7, 11, 23, 50

X

XDS Sigma 7 131